HOW TO TEACH YOUR CHILD PIANO

Even If You Can't Play Yourself!

LEVEL 2
THEORY WORKBOOK

By Stephanie Parker

Table Of Contents

Introduction:

This theory workbook is meant to be a supplement to the corresponding teaching book. Unlike the teaching book, which needs direct parent involvement, this theory book may function more independently. Coursework should assigned to your child, and then graded by you. If a student struggles to complete a theory page correctly, erase their answers and let them rework it over and over until the concept is mastered before continuing to the next chapter. Music is designed to be repetitive in its teaching for a mastery of understanding. You may see exercises repeated. This is done purposefully and will give a stronger foundation to your child's comprehension of music.

CHAPTER 1: PLAYING IN LOCATIONS NOT AT C POSITION

LESSON 1

1) Draw a C scale going up then down on the same staff

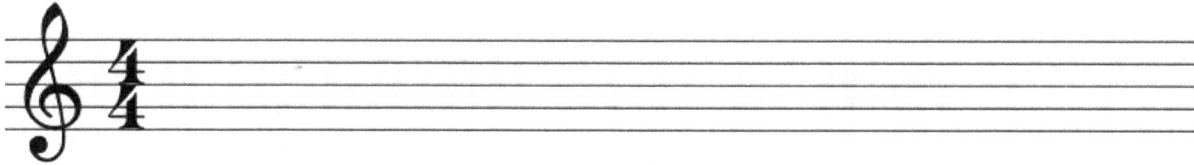

2) Write in the name of the note each note drawn.

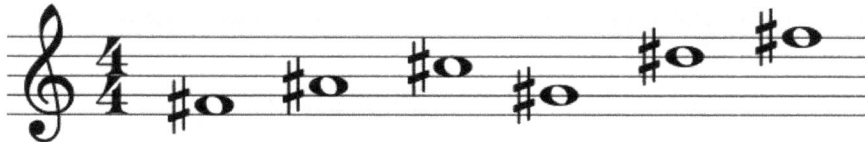

3) Write in the name of the note below each note that is drawn.

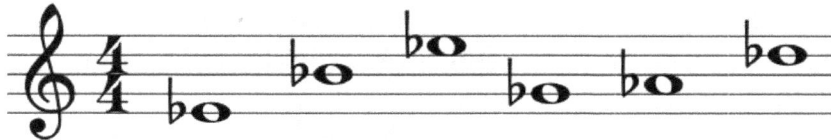

4) Draw the note that gets 1 beat _____

5). Draw the note that gets 4 beats_____

6) Draw the note that gets 3 beats _____

7) Draw the note that gets 2 beats _____

8) Draw the rest that gets 1 beat _____

9) Draw a quarter note _____

10) Draw a half note _____

11) Draw a whole note _____

12) Draw a quarter rest _____

13) Draw a dotted half note _____

14) Draw in the notes below. note: All C's refer to bass c and not middle C

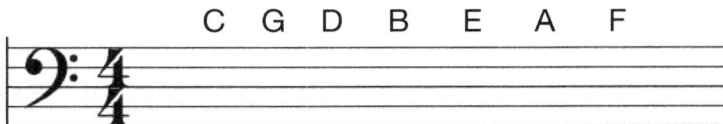

C G D B E A F

15) Draw in the notes below. note: All C's refer to treble c and not middle C

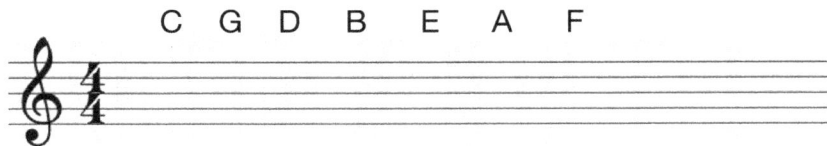

C G D B E A F

2

LESSON 2

1) Color on the piano below the correct location of the note on the image to the right.

Middle C

2) Color on the piano below the correct location of the note on the image to the right.

Middle C

3) Color on the piano below the correct location of the note on the image to the right.

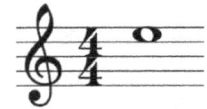

Middle C

4) Color on the piano below the correct location of the note on the image to the right.

Middle C

5) Color on the piano below the correct location of the note on the image to the right.

Middle C

LESSON 3

1) ♩ is a _____ and gets _____ beats.

2) 𝄾 is a _____ and gets _____ beat.

3) ▬ is a _____ and gets _____ beats.

4) Draw circle note heads starting on Bass C and playing the first 3 notes of the C scale (C-D-E).

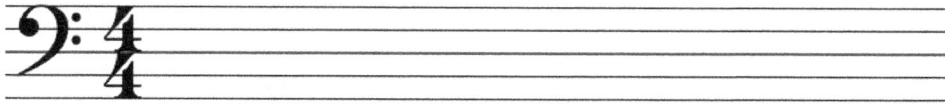

5) Write S for slur or T for tie under each example below.

6) Write S under the notes that are staccato and D under the notes that are dotted half notes.

7) Draw Space notes and then write their letter name underneath.

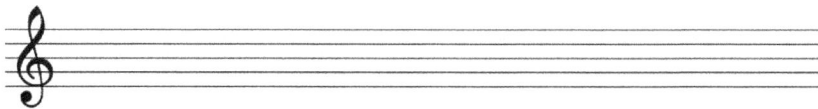

8) Draw line notes and then write their letter name underneath.

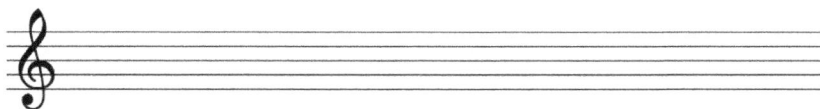

LESSON 4

1) Draw circle note heads on bass C and draw the first 5 notes of the C scale (C-D-E-F-G)

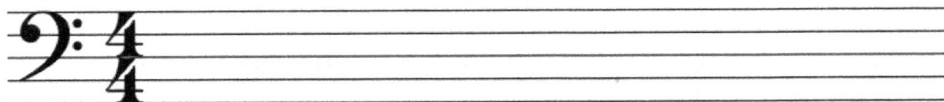

2) What is the note name of the ledger line flashcard image to the right.

3) What is the note name of the ledger line flashcard image to the right.

4) What is the note name of the ledger line flashcard image to the right

5) what is the note name of the ledger line flashcard image to the right.

6) What interval is the image to the right showing?

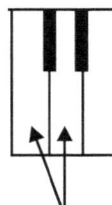

7) What interval is the image to the right showing?

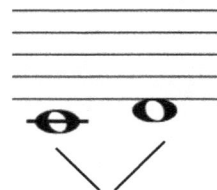

LESSON 5

1) Draw circle note heads on bass C and draw all 8 of the notes going up the C scale (C-D-E-F-G-A-B-C)

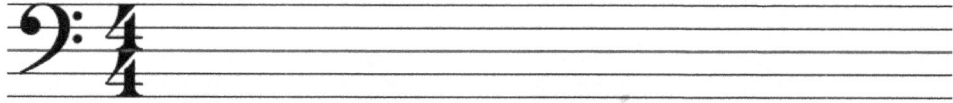

2) In the images below, write H under the half rest and W under the whole rests.

3) What interval is the image to the right showing

4) What interval is the image to the right showing

5) What interval is the image to the right showing

6) What interval is the image to the right showing

LESSON 6

1) Draw circle note heads on bass C and draw all 8 of the notes going up the C scale (C-D-E-F-G-A-B-C)

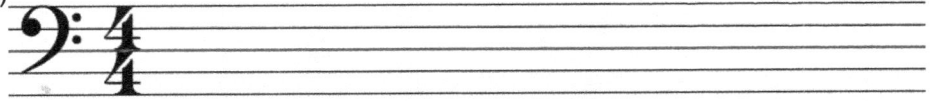

2) Draw a circle note head on the MIDDLE C and draw all 8 of the notes going DOWN the C scale

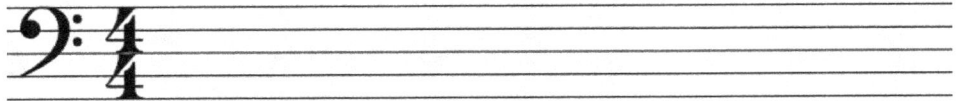

3) On one staff draw the LH C scale going up and going down the staff.

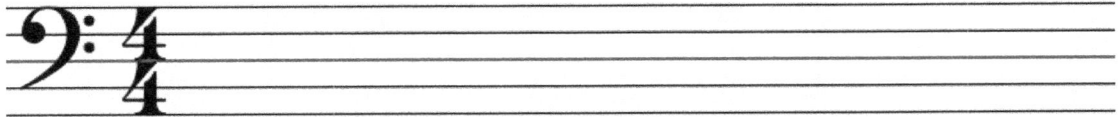

4) Draw an interval of a 2nd up from the note given.

5) Draw an interval of a 3rd up from the note given.

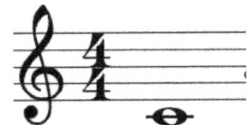

6) Color in the note note on the piano that is a 2nd up from the note the arrow is pointing to.

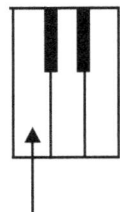

7) Color in the note on the piano that is a 3rd up from the note the arrow is pointing to.

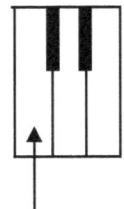

7

CHAPTER 2: The G Scale

LESSON 1

1) Draw the C scale going up and down the scale. Start at bass C, go up to middle C then go back down to bass C.

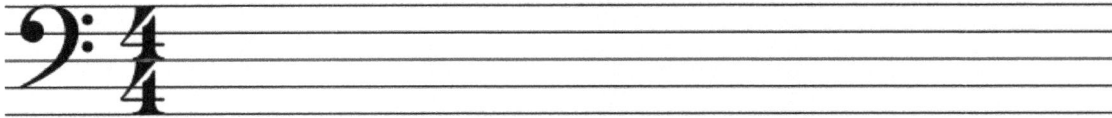

2) Draw the First three notes of the G scale in the Right hand (G-A-B).

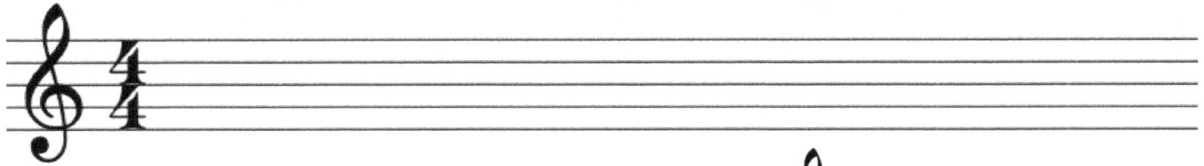

3) Draw an interval of a 2nd up from the note given.

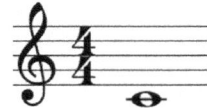

5) Draw an interval of a 3rd up from the note given.

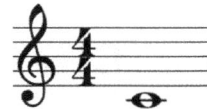

6) Draw an interval of a 4th up from the note given

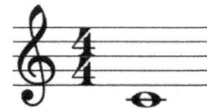

7) Color in the note note on the piano that is a 2nd up from the note the arrow is pointing to.

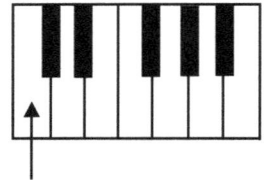

8) Color in the note on the piano that is a 3rd up from the note the arrow is pointing to.

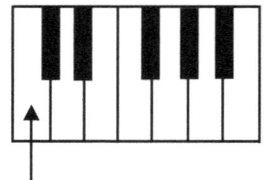

9) Color in the note on the piano that is a 4th up from the note the arrow is pointing to.

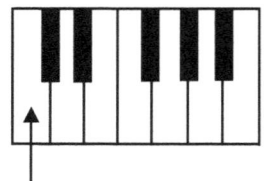

LESSON 2

2) Draw the First four notes of the G scale in the Right hand (G-A-B-C).

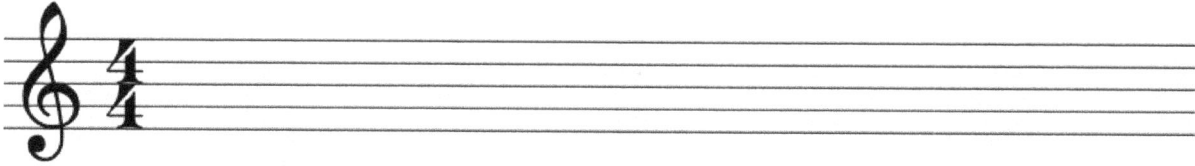

3) Draw an interval of a 2nd up from the note given.

5) Draw an interval of a 3rd up from the note given.

6) Draw an interval of a 4th up from the note given

3) Draw an interval of a 5th up from the note given

7) Color in the note note on the piano that is a 2nd up from the note the arrow is pointing to.

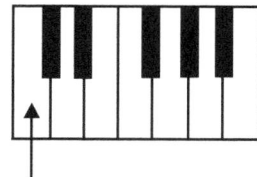

8) Color in the note on the piano that is a 3rd up from the note the arrow is pointing to.

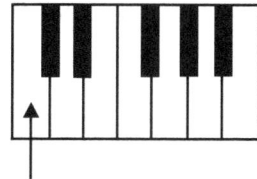

9) Color in the note on the piano that is a 4th up from the note the arrow is pointing to.

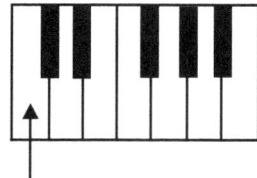

10) Color in the note on the piano that is a 5th up from the note the arrow is pointing to.

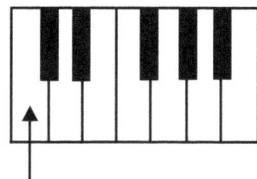

LESSON 3

1) Draw the First five notes of the G scale in the Right hand (G-A-B-C-D).

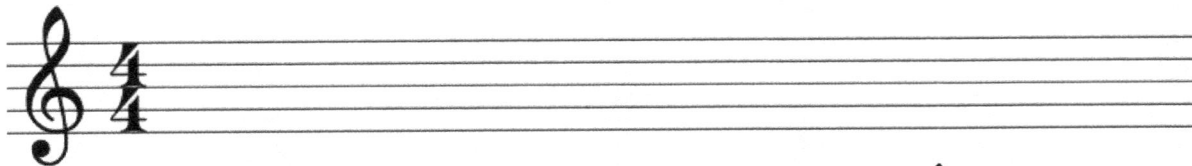

2) What interval is drawn in the image to the right.

3) What interval is drawn in the image to the right.

4) What interval is drawn in the image to the right

5) What interval is drawn in the image to the right

6) What interval are the arrows pointing to on the piano image to the right.

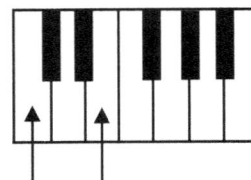

7) What interval are the arrows pointing to on the piano image to the right.

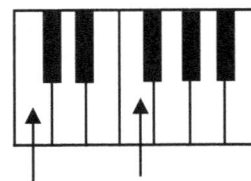

8) What interval are the arrows pointing to on the piano image to the right.

9) What interval are the arrows pointing to on the piano image to the right.

LESSON 4

1) Draw in measure bars. Then Add Staccato notes. Then write in the counts and the letter names. Then play it.

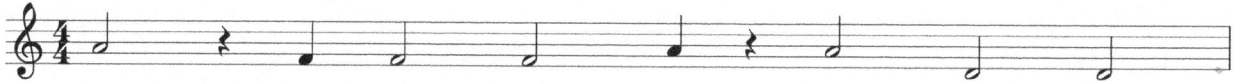

2) Remember the rule we learned that note head stems have to go either up or down and left or right based upon their location on the staff. Using that rule draw the stems correctly on each note head and name the note underneath it.

3) Draw the first six notes of the G scale in the Right hand (G-A-B-C-D-E).

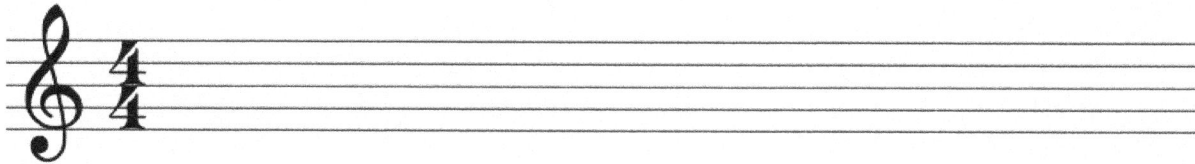

4) Draw treble C - D - E - F - G

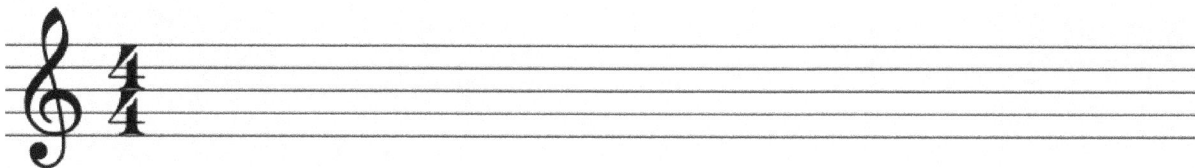

LESSON 5

1) Draw the stems correctly on each note head and name the note underneath it.

2) Draw the first seven notes of the G scale in the Right hand (G-A-B-C-D-E-F#). (When drawing a sharp on the staff, the sharp gets drawn BEFORE the note being sharped).

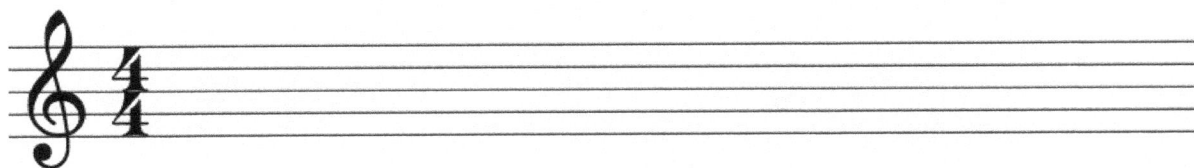

3) Write under each interval if its a 2nd, 3rd, 4th or 5th

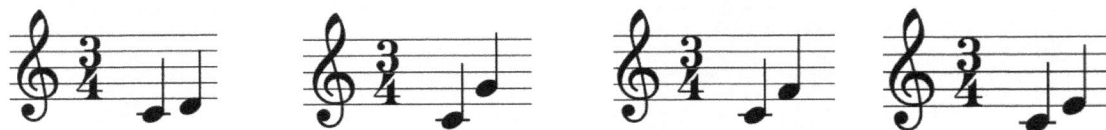

4) Write under each interval on the piano if it's a 2nd, 3rd, 4th, or 5th

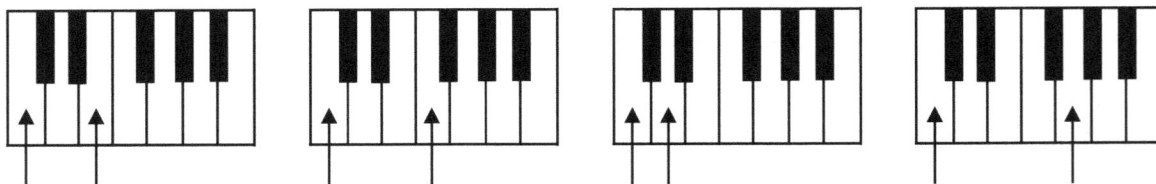

LESSON 6

1) Draw the stems correctly on each note head and name the note underneath it.

2) Draw all 8 notes of the G scale in the Right hand (G-A-B-C-D-E-F#-G). (When drawing a sharp on the staff, the sharp gets drawn BEFORE the note being sharped).

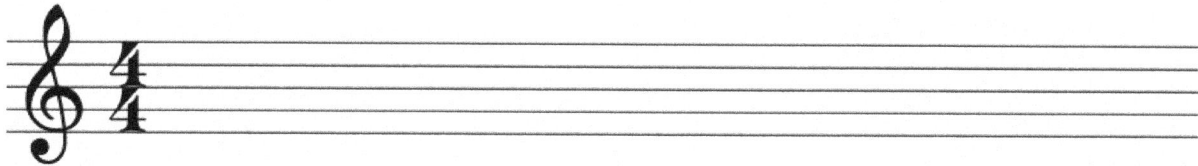

3) Draw in measure bars. Then Add Staccato notes. Then write in the counts and the letter names. Then play it.

4) Draw treble C - D - E - F - G

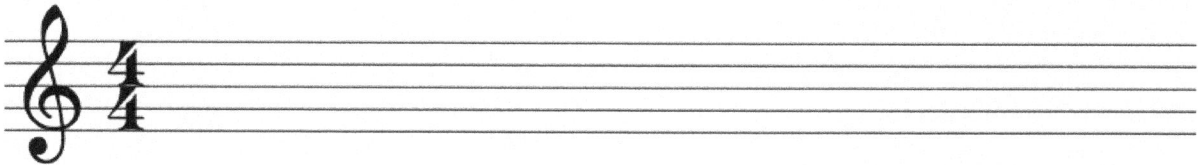

5) Color the note a 2nd above the note with the arrow.

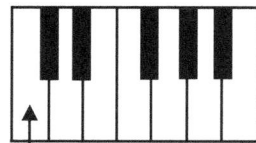

6) Color the note a 5th above the note with the arrow.

7) Color the note a 4th above the note with the arrow.

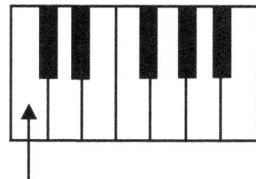

CHAPTER 3: Learning Major Chords

LESSON 1

1) COLOR THE BASS C ON THE PIANO BELOW

MIDDLE C

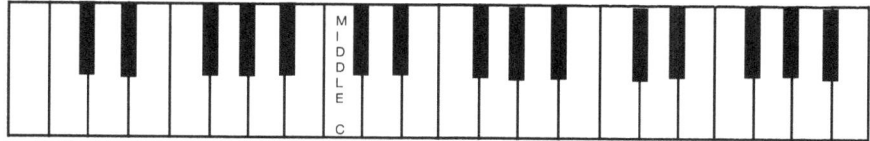

2) COLOR THE TREBLE C ON THE PIANO BELOW

MIDDLE C

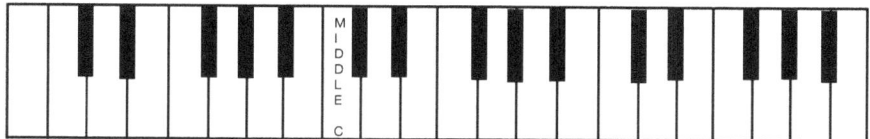

3) COLOR THE NOTES THAT MAKE UP A C MAJOR CHORDON THE PIANO TO THE RIGHT.

4) BASED ON THE FLASHCARD IMAGE TO THE RIGHT, COLOR THE SAME NOTE ON THE PIANO BELOW.

MIDDLE

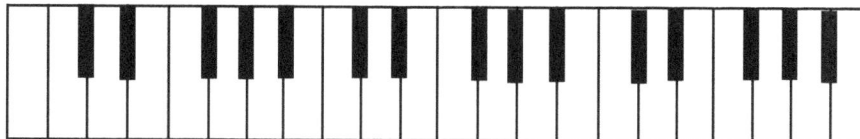

5) BASED ON THE FLASHCARD IMAGE TO THE RIGHT, COLOR THE SAME NOTE ON THE PIANO BELOW.

MIDDLE

6) BASED ON THE FLASHCARD IMAGE TO THE RIGHT, COLOR THE SAME NOTE ON THE PIANO BELOW.

MIDDLE

LESSON 2

1) Draw all 8 notes in the right hand G scale going (G-A-B-C-D-E-F#-G). Then draw 1 additional note going down (G-F#)

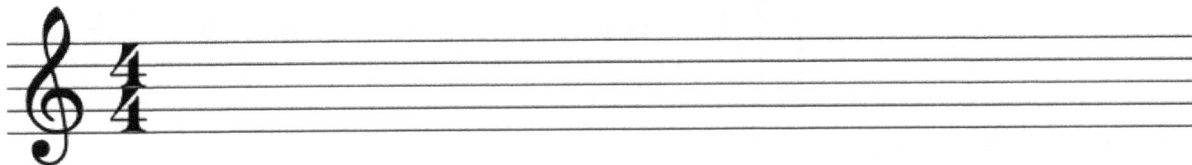

2) What is the letter name of the ledger line flashcard to the right.

3) What is the letter name of the ledger line flashcard to the right.

4) What is the letter name of the ledger line flashcard to the right.

5) What is the letter name of the ledger line flashcard to the right.

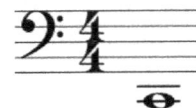

6) Color the note that is an interval of a 3rd above the note with the arrow.

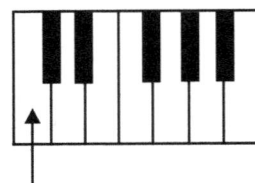

7) Color the note that is an interval of a 5th above the note with the arrow.

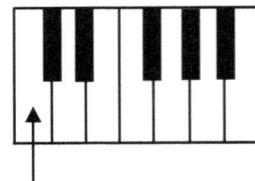

8) Color the note that is an interval of a 4th above the note with the arrow.

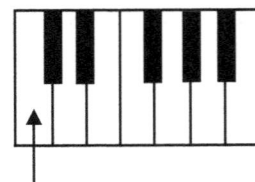

LESSON 3

1) Draw all 8 notes in the right hand G scale going up and 1 note going down (G-A-B-C-D-E-F#-G). Then draw 2 additional notes going down (G-F#-E)

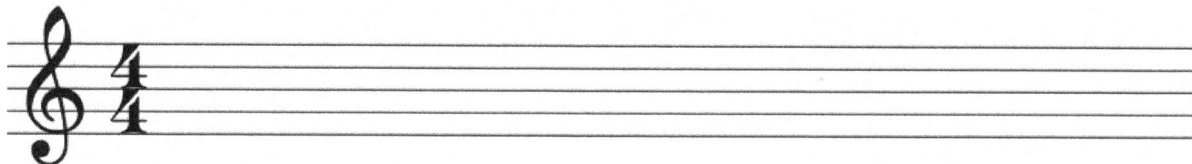

2) Write the name of the chord drawn on the piano image to the right.

3) Write the name of the chord drawn on the piano image to the right.

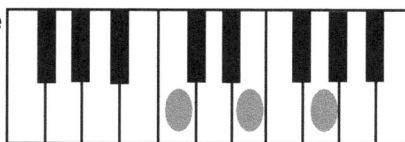

4) Write under each interval whether its a 2nd, 3rd, 4th or 5th

5) Color the notes that make up the F major chord.

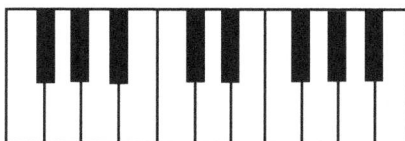

6) Color the notes that make up the C Major chord.

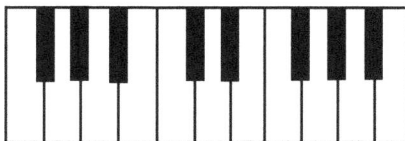

7) Write the letter of each note underneath each flashcard.

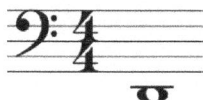

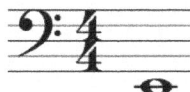

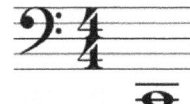

LESSON 4

1) Write the letter of each note underneath each flashcard.

2) Draw all 8 notes in the right hand G scale going up (G-A-B-C-D-E-F#-G). Then draw 3 additional notes going down (G-F#-E-D).

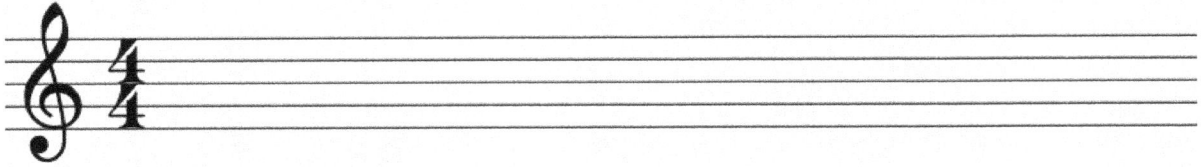

3) Draw the stems correctly on each note head and name the note underneath it.

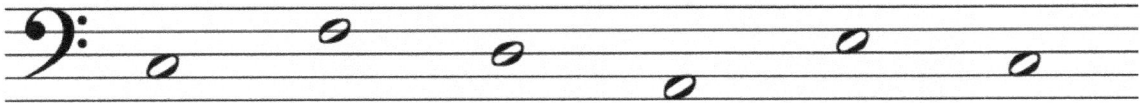

4) Draw in measure bars. Then Add Staccato notes. Then write in the counts and the letter names. Then play it.

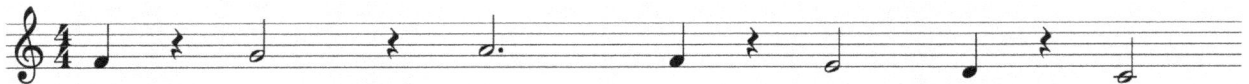

LESSON 5

1) Draw all 8 notes in the right hand G scale going up (G-A-B-C-D-E-F#-G). Then draw 5 additional notes going down (G-F#-E-D-C-B).

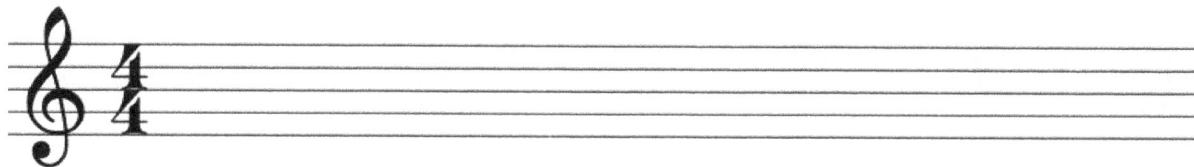

2) Color the notes that make up the C major chord.

3) Color the notes that make up the F Major chord.

4) Color the notes that make up the G Major chord.

5) Color the note that is an interval of a 3rd above the note with the arrow.

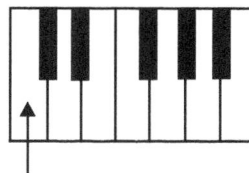

6) Color the note that is an interval of a 5th above the note with the arrow.

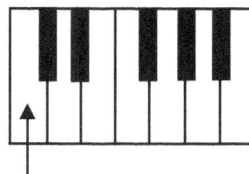

7) Color the note that is an interval of a 4th above the note with the arrow.

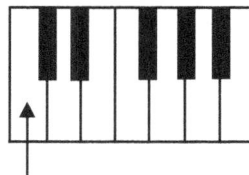

8) Color the note that is an interval of a 2nd above the note with the arrow.

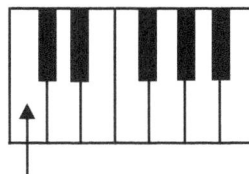

LESSON 6

1) Draw all 8 notes in the right hand G scale going up and 3 note going down (G-A-B-C-D-E-F#-G). Then draw all 8 notes going down (G-F#-E-D-C-B-A-G).

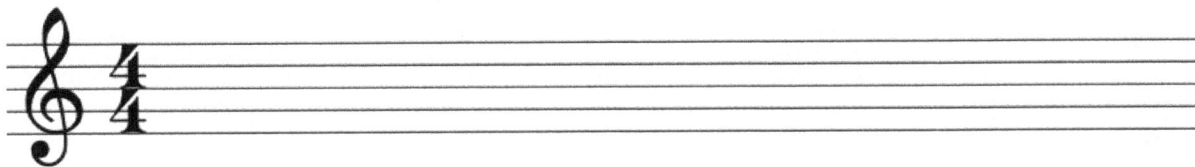

2) Write the letter of each note underneath each flashcard.

3) Write the name of the chord you see drawn on the piano image to the right

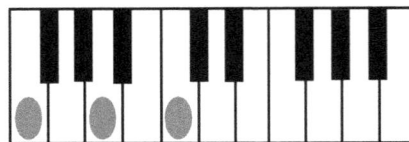

4) Write the name of the chord you see drawn on the piano image to the right

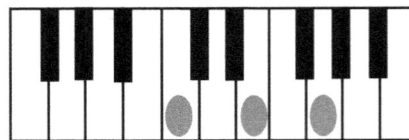

5) Write the name of the chord you see drawn on the piano image to the right

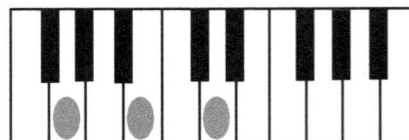

6) In the images below, write H under the half rest and W under the whole rests.

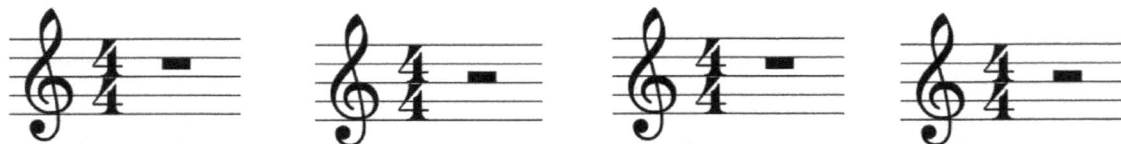

CHAPTER 4: More Major Chords and Playing 8va.

LESSON 1

1) Circle on the piano image a C#

2) Circle on the piano image a F#

3) Circle on the piano image a D #

4) Circle on the piano image an A #

5) Circle on the piano image a B-flat

6) Circle on the piano image a D-flat

7) Circle on the piano image a G-flat

8) Circle on the piano image an A-flat

LESSON 2

1) Write the C major scale going up and down the scale

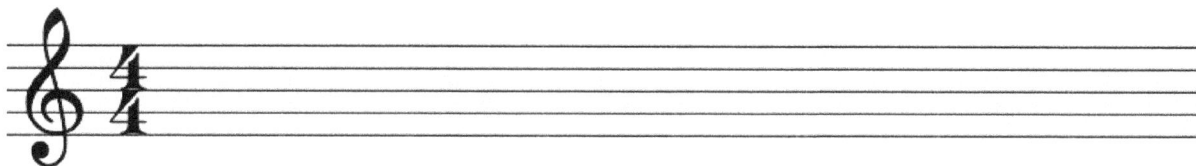

2) Write the G major scale going up and down the scale

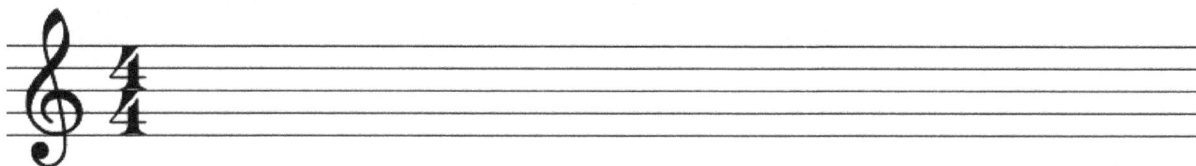

3) Color the note on the piano below in the correct location that the music shows

4) Color the note on the piano below in the correct location that the music shows

5) Color the note on the piano below in the correct location that the music shows

6) Draw a C major chord on the staff. Remember the bottom note should be the name of the chord and then the rest of the chord is skips.

LESSON 3

1) Color the note on the piano below in the correct location that the music shows

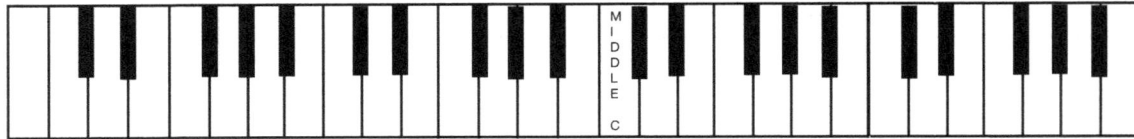

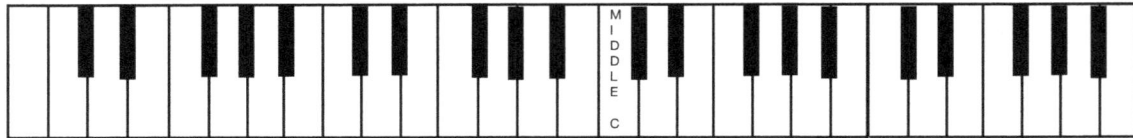

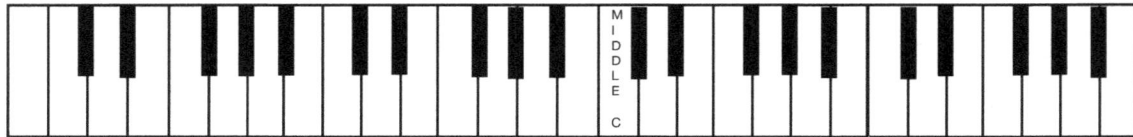

2) Color the note on the piano below in the correct location that the music shows

3) Color the note on the piano below in the correct location that the music shows

4) Draw a whole rest in each measure (Remember the whole rest hangs down from the 4th line

5) Draw two half rests in each measure (Remember the half rest sits above the 3rd line)

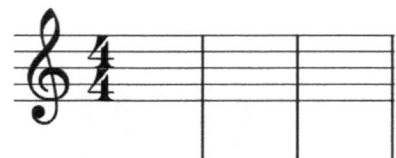

6) Draw a F major chord on the staff. Remember the bottom note should be the name of the chord and then the rest of the chord is skips

LESSON 4

1) Color the note on the piano below in the correct location that the music shows.

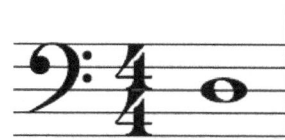

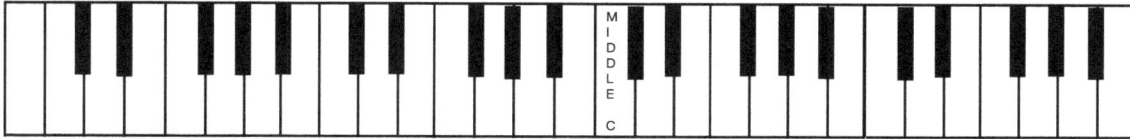

2) Color the note on the piano below in the correct location that the music shows

3) Color the note on the piano below in the correct location that the music shows

4) Draw whole rests in each measure in the treble clef (Remember the whole rest hangs down from the 4th line) and two half rests in each measure in the bass clef (Remember the half rest sits above the 3rd line)

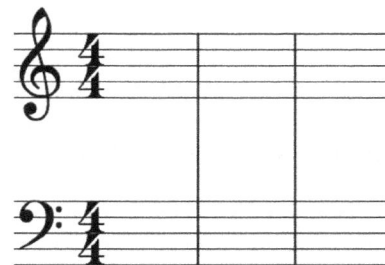

5) Draw a G major chord on the staff. Remember the bottom note should be the name of the chord and then the rest of the chord is skips

LESSON 5

1) Identify the name of the chord you see drawn in the image to the right

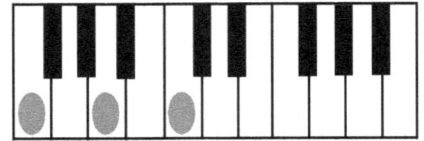

2) Identify the name of the chord you see drawn in the image to the right

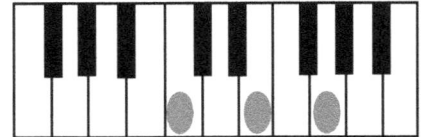

3) Identify the name of the chord you see drawn in the image to the right

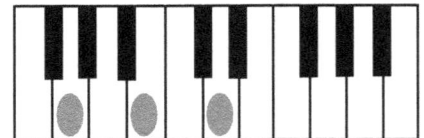

4) Identify the name of the chord you see drawn in the image to the right

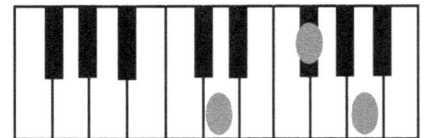

5) Identify the name of the chord you see drawn in the image to the right

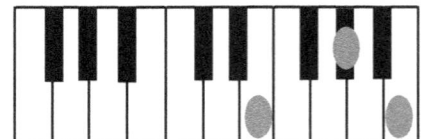

6) Identify the name of the chord you see drawn in the image to the right

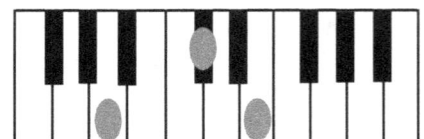

CHAPTER 5: Playing Sharps and Flats

LESSON 1

1) What are the black notes if any in the C scale?

2) What are the black notes if any in the G scale?

3) What are the black notes in the D scale

4) Draw the first 2 notes in the right hand D scale going up (D-E)

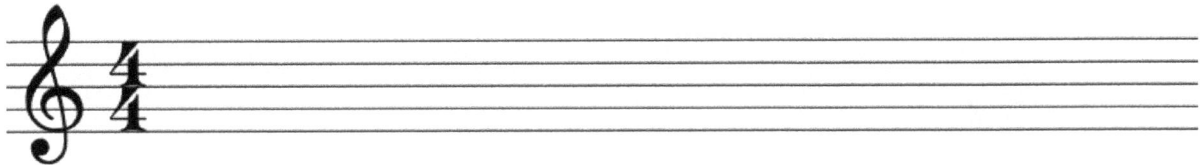

5) Color the note on the piano image to the right that is an interval of a 3rd BELOW the note with the arrow.

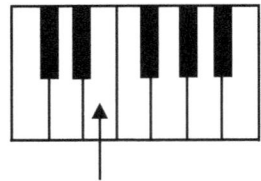

6) Color the note on the piano image to the right that is an interval of a 5th BELOW the note with the arrow.

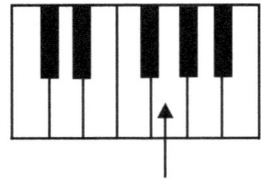

7) Color the note on the piano image to the right that is an interval of a 4th BELOW the note with the arrow.

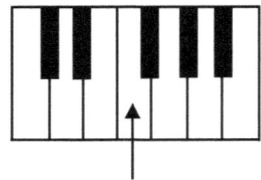

8) Color the note on the piano image to the right that is an interval of a 2nd BELOW the note with the arrow.

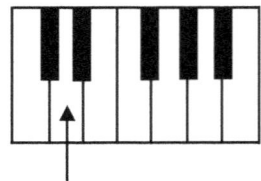

LESSON 2

1) What scale has 2 black notes?

2) What scale has 0 black notes?

3) what scale has 1 black notes?

4) Draw the first 3 notes in the right hand D scale going up (D-E-F#)

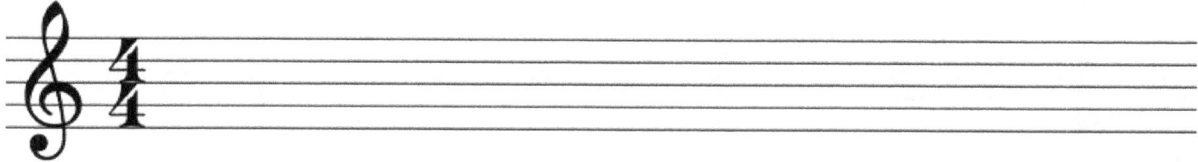

5) Draw an note an interval of a 2nd DOWN from the note in the image to the right.

6) Draw an note an interval of a 5th DOWN from the note in the image to the right.

7) Draw an note an interval of a 3rd DOWN from the note in the image to the right.

8) Draw an note an interval of a 4th DOWN from the note in the image to the right.

LESSON 3

1) What scale has the black note F#

2) What scale has no black notes

3) What scale has the black notes F# and C#

4) Draw the first 5 notes on the RH D scale going up (D-E-F#-G-A)

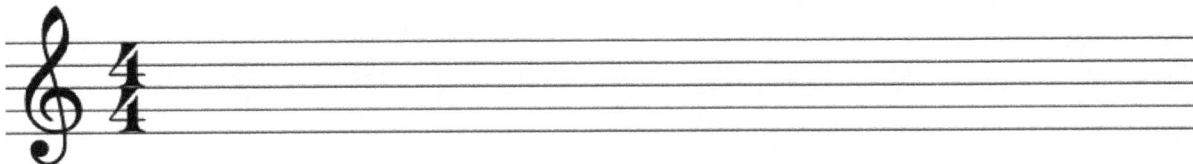

5) 5) Draw in the missing sharps (#) in the scale drawn below. Remember when we draw a sharp on a staff it comes BEFORE the note being sharped.

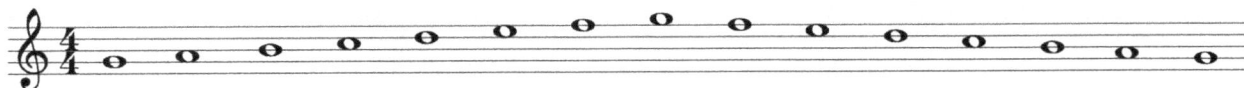

6) Color the note on the piano below in the correct location that the music shows.

7) Color the note on the piano below in the correct location that the music shows.

LESSON 4

1) What scale is written in the image below?

2) Write the name of the note underneath each flashcard.

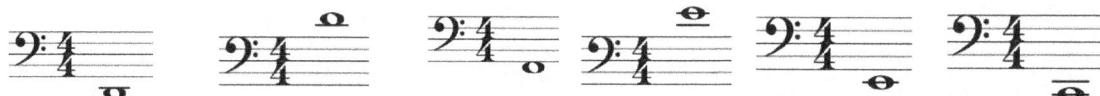

3 Draw the first 6 notes of the RH D scale going up (D-E-F#-G-A-B)

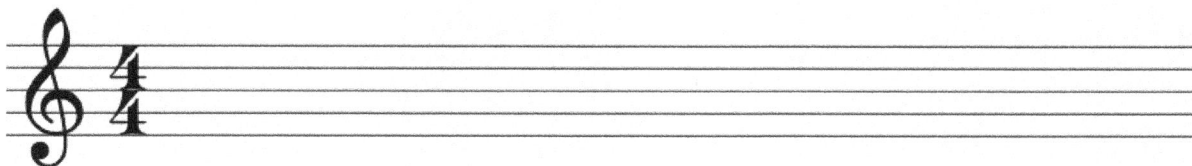

4 6) Circle on the piano image a D #

7) Circle on the piano image a A flat

8) Circle on the piano image an G#

LESSON 5

1) What scale is written in the image below?

2) Circle on the piano image a G-flat

2) Circle on the piano image a F#

3) Circle on the piano image a E-flat

4) Circle on the piano image an A #

5) Circle on the piano image a B-flat

6) Draw the first 7 notes of the RH D scale going up (D-E-F#-G-A-B-C#)

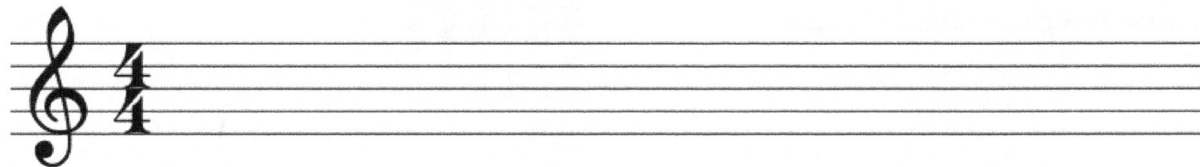

LESSON 6

1) What scale is written in the image below?

2) Identify the name of the chord you see drawn in the image to the right

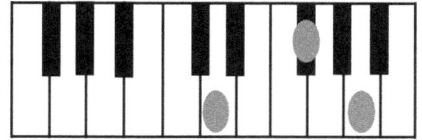

2) Identify the name of the chord you see drawn in the image to the right

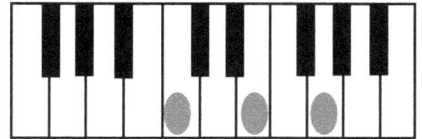

3) Identify the name of the chord you see drawn in the image to the right

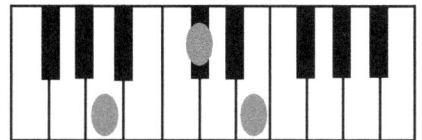

4) Identify the name of the chord you see drawn in the image to the right

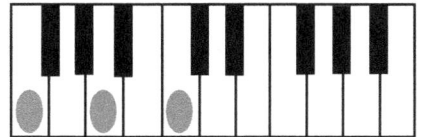

5) Identify the name of the chord you see drawn in the image to the right

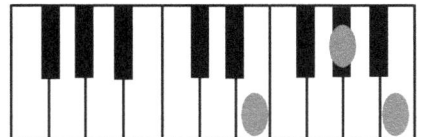

6) Identify the name of the chord you see drawn in the image to the right.

7) Draw all 8 notes of the RH D scale going up (D-E-F#-G-A-B-C#-D)

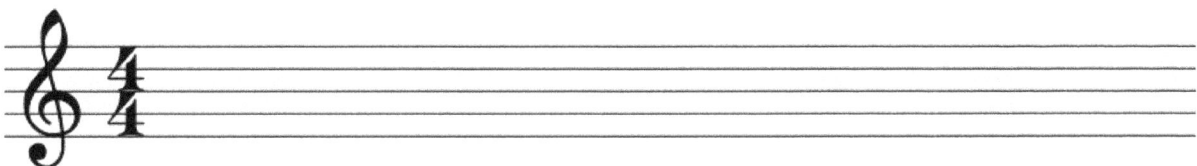

CHAPTER 6: Playing Chords in Music

LESSON 1

1) Shade in the notes in the correct location on the piano below the chord in the image to the right.

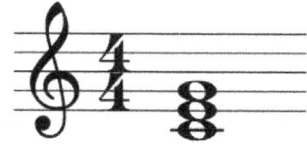

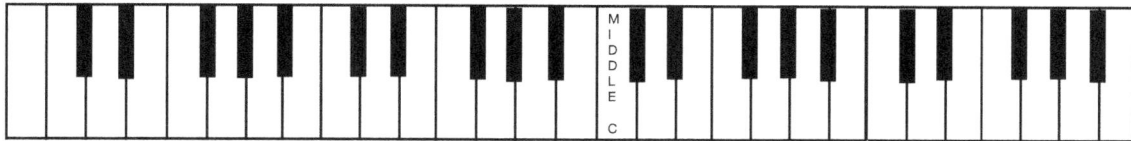

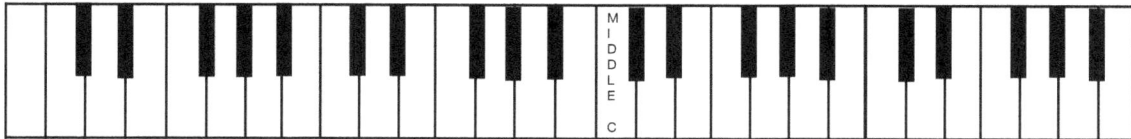

2) Shade in the notes in the correct location on the piano below the chord in the image to the right.

3). Draw all 8 notes in the right hand D scale going up (D-E-F#-G-A-B-C#-D). Then draw 1 additional note going down (D-C#).

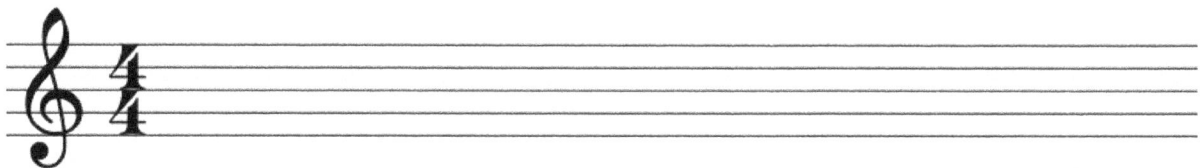

4) Write the name of each note underneath the note.

LESSON 2

1) Shade in the notes in the correct location on the piano below the chord in the image to the right.

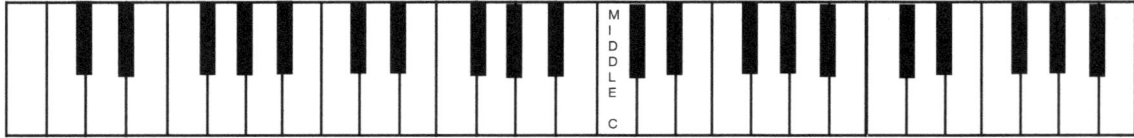

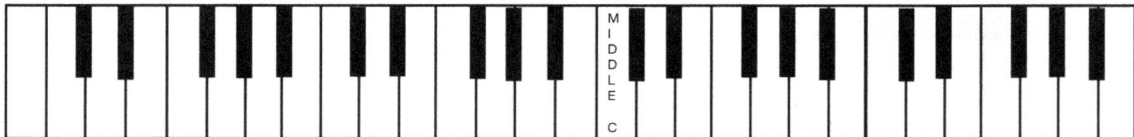

2) Shade in the notes in the correct location on the piano below the chord in the image to the right.

3) Draw all 8 notes in the right hand D scale going up (D-E-F#-G-A-B-C#-D). Then draw 3 additional notes going down (D-C#-B-A).

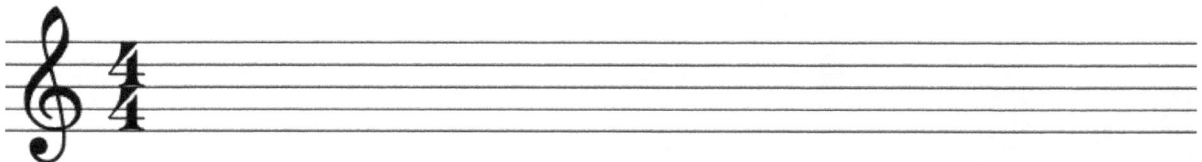

4) Write the name of each note underneath the note.

LESSON 3

1) Shade in the notes in the correct location on the piano below the chord in the image to the right.

2) Shade in the notes in the correct location on the piano below the chord in the image to the right.

3) Draw all 8 notes in the right hand D scale going up (D-E-F#-G-A-B-C#-D). Then draw 5 additional notes going down (D-C#-B-A-G-F#).

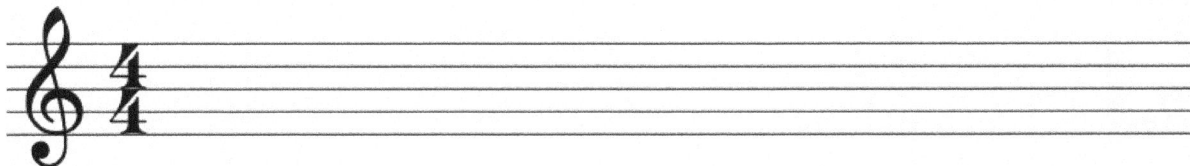

4) Draw the note that gets 1 beat _____

5). Draw the note that gets 4 beats_____

6) Draw the note that gets 3 beats _____

7) Draw the note that gets 2 beats _____

8) Draw the rest that gets 1 beat _____

9) Draw a quarter note _____

10) Draw a half note _____

11) Draw a whole note _____

12) Draw a quarter rest _____

13) Draw a dotted half note _____

LESSON 4

1) Shade in the notes in the correct location on the piano below the chord in the image to the right.

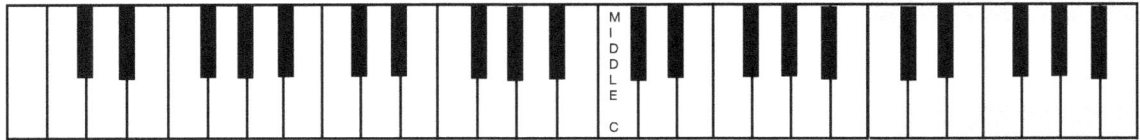

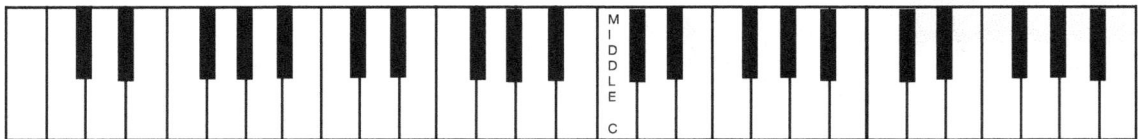

2) Shade in the notes in the correct location on the piano below the chord in the image to the right.

3) Draw all 8 notes in the right hand D scale going up (D-E-F#-G-A-B-C#-D). Then draw all 8 additional notes going down (D-C#-B-A-G-F#-E-D).

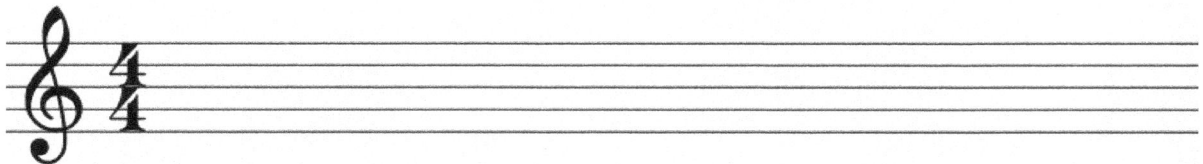

4) Draw in measure bars. Then Add Staccato notes. Then write in the counts and the letter names. Then play it.

LESSON 5

1) Shade in the notes in the correct location on the piano below the chord in the image to the right.

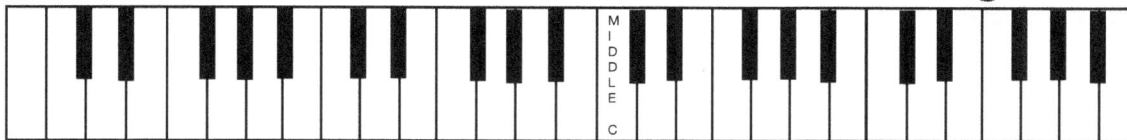

2) Shade in the notes in the correct location on the piano below the chord in the image to the right.

3) Draw the C scale going up and Down in the right hand. Underneath each note write the finger number that plays that note.

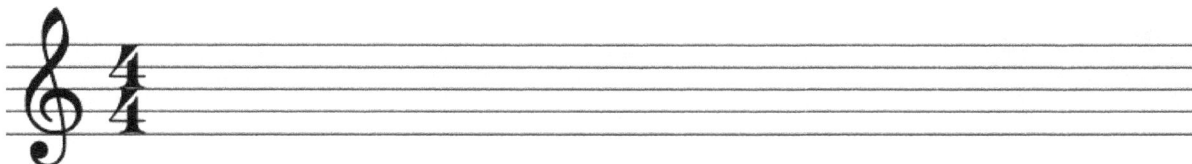

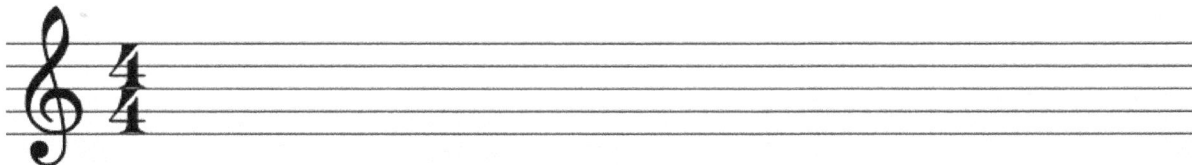

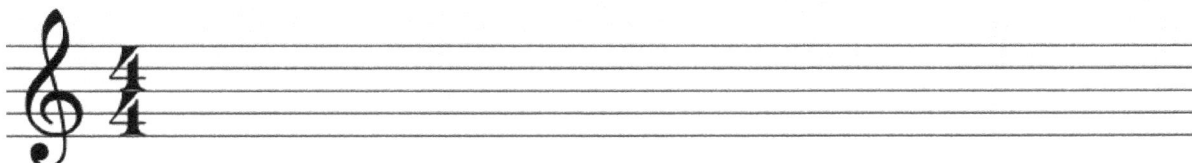

4) Draw that G scale going up and Down in the right hand. Underneath each note write the finger number that plays that note.

5) Draw the D scale going up and down in the right hand. Underneath each note write the finger number that plays that note.

LESSON 6

1) Shade in the notes in the correct location on the piano below the chord in the image to the right.

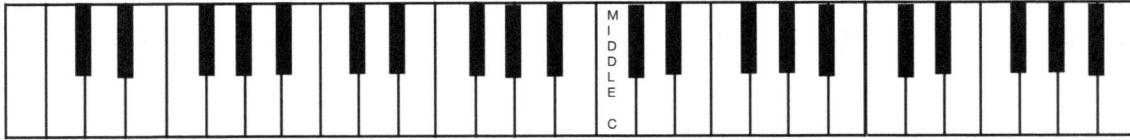

2) Shade in the notes in the correct location on the piano below the chord in the image to the right.

3) Draw the C scale going up and Down in the left hand. Underneath each note write the finger number that plays that note.

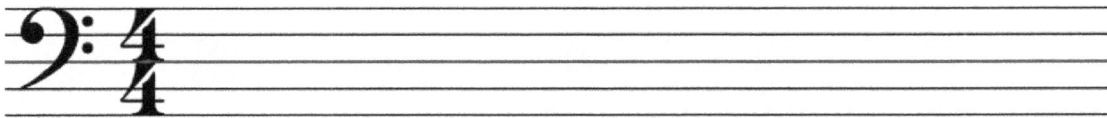

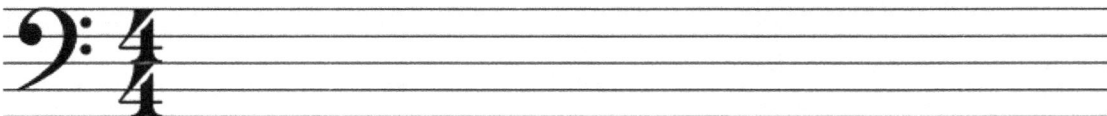

4) Draw that G scale going up and Down in the left hand. Underneath each note write the finger number that plays that note.

5) Add measure bars. Draw in staccato note where applicable. Then write in the counts and letter names and play it.

CHAPTER 7: Practicing Major Chords

LESSON 1

1) Draw the stems correctly on each note head and write the note name underneath it.

2) Identify in each image below if it is an interval of a 2nd, 3rd, 4th or 5th. Than play that interval on the piano.

3) Identify the interval indicated by the arrows on each piano below (2nd, 3rd, 4th, 5th).

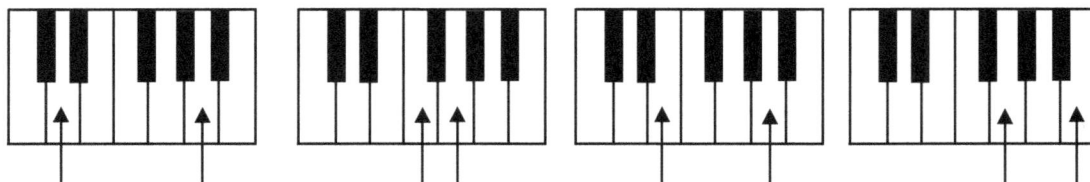

4) Draw the first 3 notes in the F Scale in the RH going up (F-G-A).

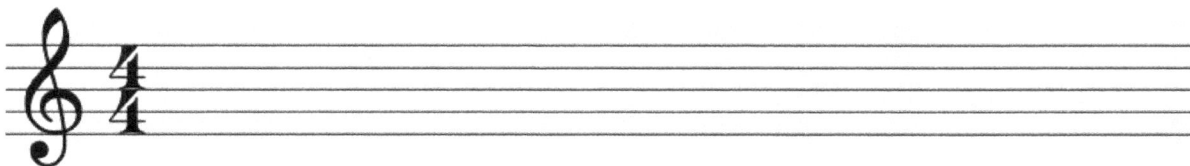

5) Draw in the missing bar lines. Write in the counts and note names. Play the song on the piano.

LESSON 2

1) Draw an interval of a 4th going up starting from a D note.

2) Draw an interval of a 3rd going up starting from a F note.

3) Draw an interval of a 5th going up starting from a E note.

4) Draw an interval of a 2nd going up starting from a G note.

5) Draw the stems correctly on each note head and write the note name underneath it.

6) Draw the first 4 notes of the F scale in the RH going up (F-G-A-B♭).

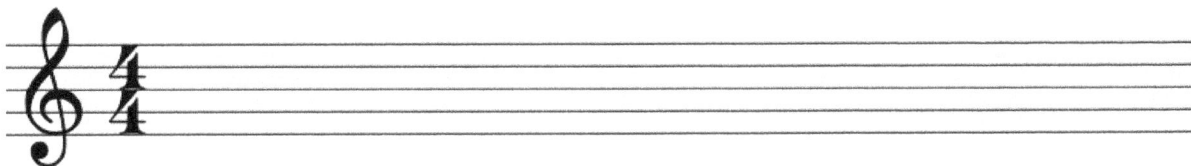

LESSON 3

1) Draw an interval of a 3rd up from the note in the image to the right then play the two notes on a piano.

2) Draw an interval of a 4th up from the note in the image to the right then play the two notes on a piano.

3) Draw an interval of a 2nd up from the note in the image to the right then play the two notes on a piano.

4) Draw an interval of a 5th up from the note in the image to the right then play the two notes on a piano.

5) Draw the first 5 notes of the F scale in the RH going up (F-G-A-B♭-C).

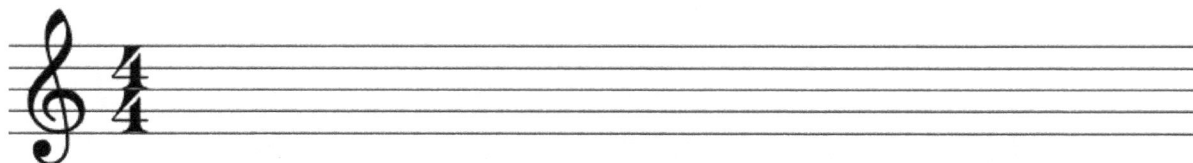

6) Draw the missing bar lines. Write in the counts and note names. Play the music.

LESSON 4

1) What is the interval you see drawn in the image to the right?

2) What is the interval you see drawn in the image to the right?

3) What is the interval you see drawn in the image to the right?

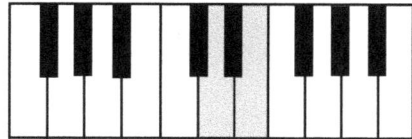

4) What is the interval you see drawn in the image to the right?

5) Draw all 8 notes of the F scale in the RH going up (F-G-A-B♭-C-D-E-F).

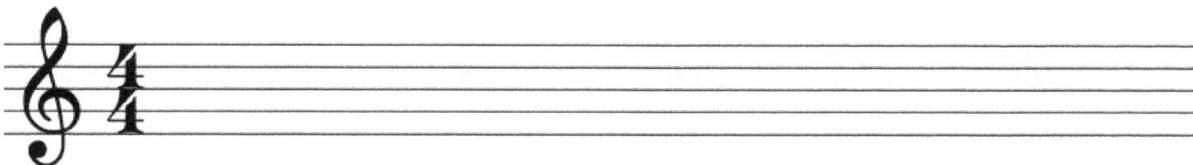

6) Draw in the missing bar lines for the GRAND STAFF below. Write in the counts and note names. Play the music.

LESSON 5

1) Draw all 8 notes of the F scale in the RH going up (F-G-A-B♭-C-D-E-F), then draw 3 additional notes going down (E-D-C).

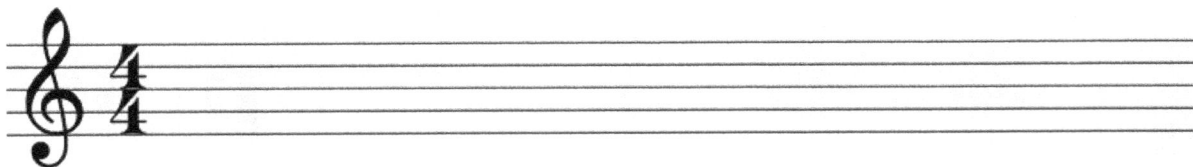

2) Write the note name of the flashcard in each image below.

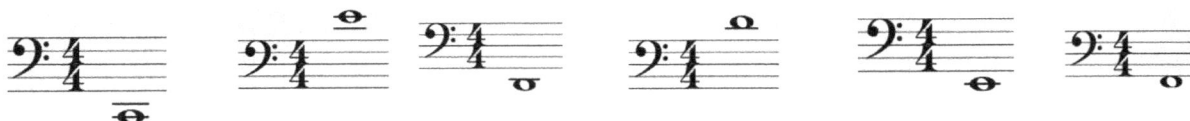

3) Write the note name of the flashcard in each image below.

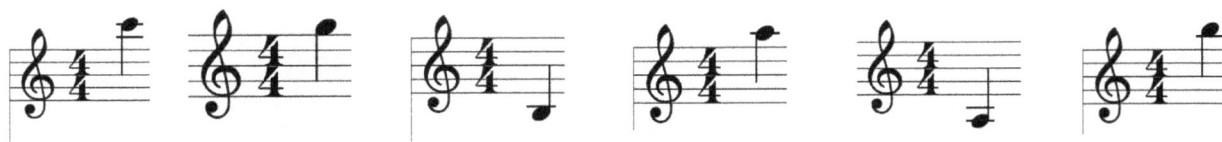

4) Draw an interval of a 2nd down from the note in the image to the right. Then play the two notes on the piano.

5) Draw an interval of a 3rd down from the note in the image to the right. Then play the two notes on the piano.

6) Draw an interval of a 5th down from the note In the image to the right. Then play the two notes on the piano.

7) Draw an interval of a 4th down from the note in the image to the right. Then play the two notes on the piano.

LESSON 6

1) Draw all 8 notes of the F scale in the RH going up (F-G-A-B♭-C-D-E-F), then draw 4 additional notes going down (E-D-C-B♭).

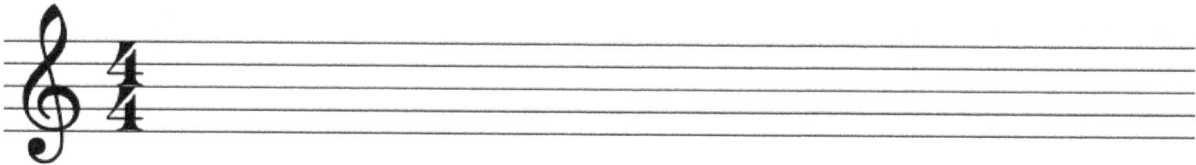

2) Color the white notes and draw a circle on any black notes in a C chord

3) Color the white notes and draw a circle any black notes in a D Chord

4) Color the white notes and draw a circle on any black notes in an E chord

5) Color the white notes and draw a circle on any black notes a F chord

6) Color the white notes and draw a circle on any black notes in a G chord

7) Color the white notes and draw a circle on any black notes in an A chord.

CHAPTER 8: Putting It All Together

LESSON 1

1) Draw all 8 notes of the F scale in the RH going up (F-G-A-B♭-C-D-E-F), then draw all 8 notes going down (F-E-D-C-B♭-A-G-F).

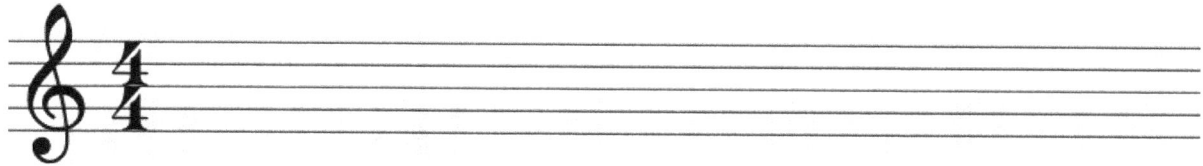

2) On the piano below, color the note in the correct location that the LH would play and draw an arrow pointing to the correct location that the RH would play on the image to the right.

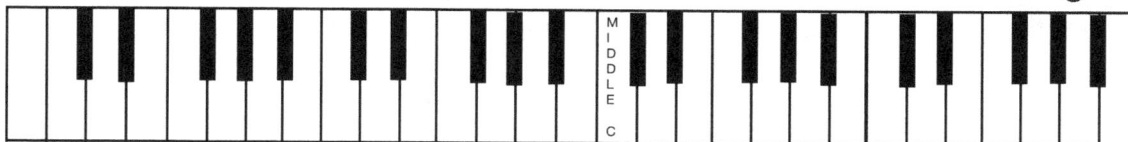

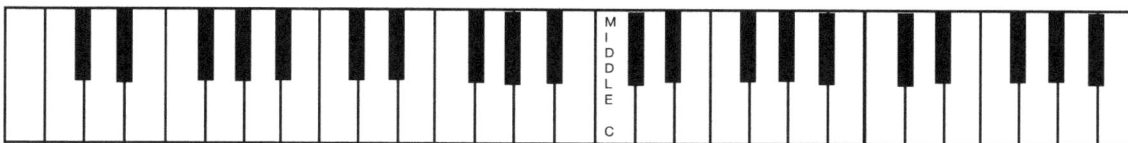

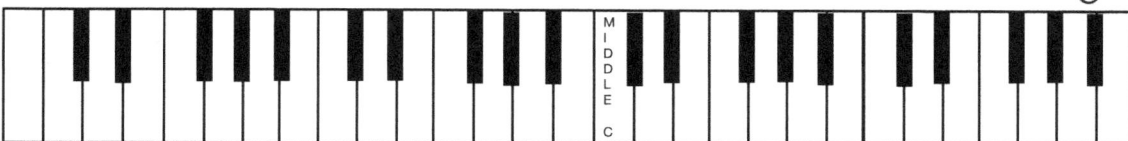

3) On the piano below, color the note in the correct location that the LH would play and draw an arrow pointing to the correct location that the RH would play on the image to the right.

4) On the piano below, color the note in the correct location that the LH would play and draw an arrow pointing to the correct location that the RH would play on the image to the right.

LESSON 2

1) On the piano below, color the note in the correct location that the LH would play and draw an arrow pointing to the correct location that the RH would play based on the image to the right.

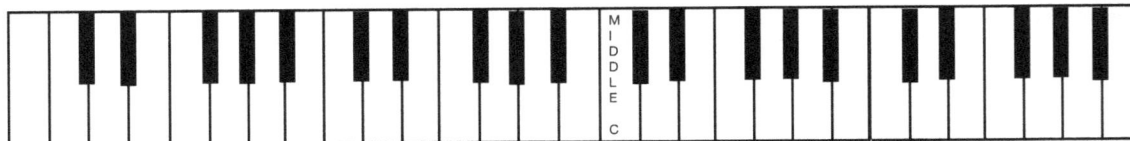

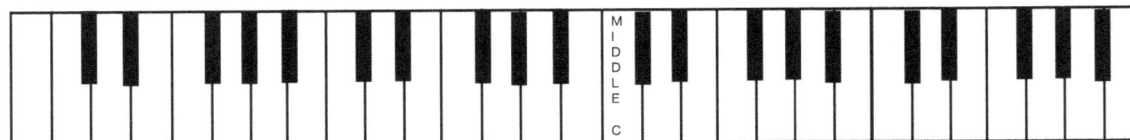

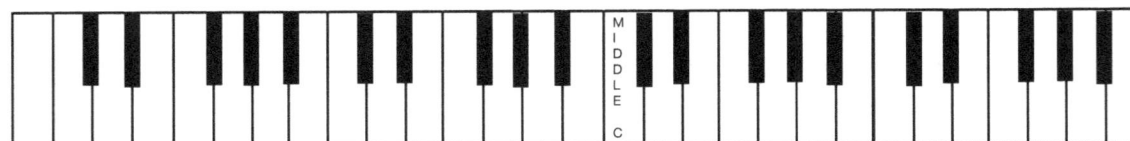

2) On the piano below, color the note in the correct location that the LH would play and draw an arrow pointing to the correct location that the RH would play based on the image to the right.

3) On the piano below, color the note in the correct location that the LH would play and draw an arrow pointing to the correct location that the RH would play based on the image to the right.

4) Draw a F scale in the RH going up and down. Include the finger numbers on each note.

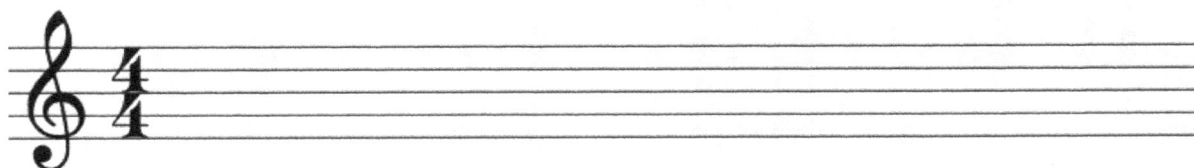

51

LESSON 3

1) Draw a C scale in the RH going up and down with finger numbers underneath.

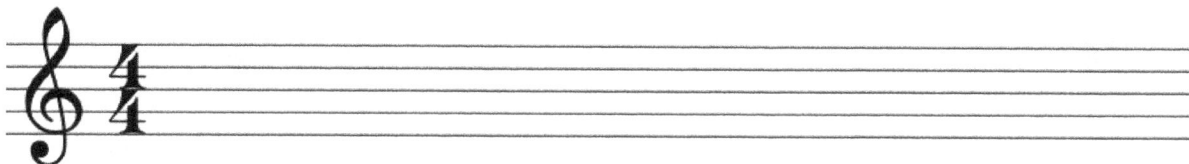

2) Draw a G scale in the RH going up and down with the finger numbers underneath.

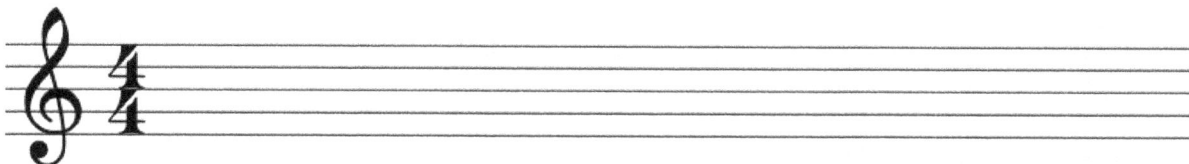

3) Draw a D scale in the RH going up and down with the finger numbers underneath.

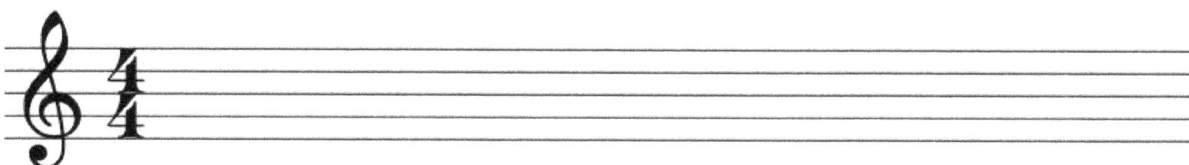

4) Draw a F scale in the RH going up and down with the finger numbers underneath.

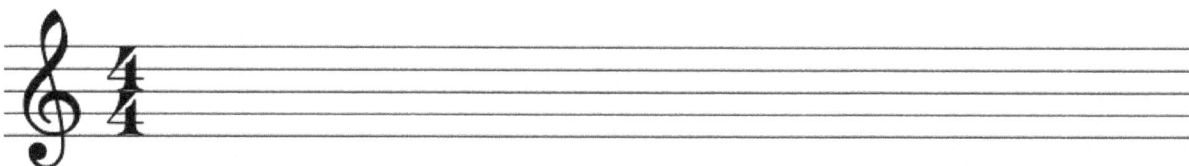

5) Color the correct location on the piano for the image to the right.

6) Color the correct location on the piano for the image to the right.

LESSON 4

1) What if any are the black notes in the D Scale?

2) What if any are the black notes in the C scale?

3) What if any are the black notes in the G scale?

4) What if any are the black notes in the F scale?

5) What three major chords use all white notes?

6) What three major chords have a black note in the middle?

7) What major chord uses 2 black notes?

8) What does Rit. Stand for and what is its definition?

9) Draw a fermata and give its definition.

10) What term does *mp* stand for and what does it mean?

11) Draw a whole rest and tell how many beats.

12) Draw a half rest and tell how many beats.

13) What does 8va mean?

14) What are the notes in a C major chord?

15) What are the notes in a D major chord?

16) What are the notes in an E major chord?

17) What are the notes in a F major chord?

18) What are the notes in a G major chord?

19) What are the notes in an A major chord?

20) What are the notes in a B major chord?

ANSWER KEY

Chapter 1: Playing in Locations not at C Position

LESSON 1

1) Draw a C scale going up then down on the same staff

2) Write in the name of the note below each note drawn.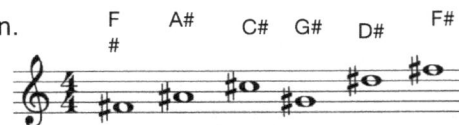

3) Write in the name of the note below each note that is drawn.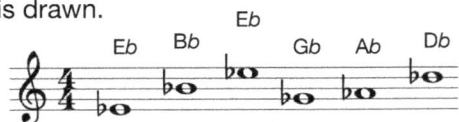

4) Draw the note that gets 1 beat _____

5). Draw the note that gets 4 beats _____

6) Draw the note that gets 3 beats _____

7) Draw the note that gets 2 beats _____

8) Draw the rest that gets 1 beat _____

9) Draw a quarter note _____

10) Draw a half note _____

11) Draw a whole note _____

12) Draw a quarter rest _____

13) Draw a dotted half note _____

14) Draw in the notes below. note: All C's refer to bass c and not middle C. Answers may vary on notes that have two locations on the staff.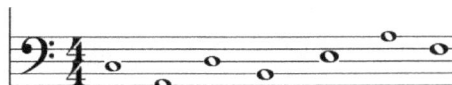

15) Draw in the notes below. note: All C's refer to treble c and not middle C. Answers may vary on notes that have two locations on the staff

LESSON 2

1) Color on the piano below the correct location of the note on the image to the right.

Middle C

2) Color on the piano below the correct location of the note on the image to the right.

Middle C

3) Color on the piano below the correct location of the note on the image to the right.

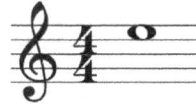

Middle C

4) Color on the piano below the correct location of the note on the image to the right.

Middle C

5) Color on the piano below the correct location of the note on the image to the right.

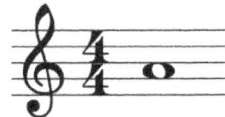

Middle C

LESSON 3

1) ▬ is a ____Half Rest__ and gets ___2___ beats.

2) 𝄽 is a ____Quarter Rest__ and gets __1____ beat.

3) ▬ is a ___Whole Rest_____ and gets ___4____ beats.

4) Draw circle note heads starting on Bass C and playing the first 3 notes of the C scale (C-D-E).

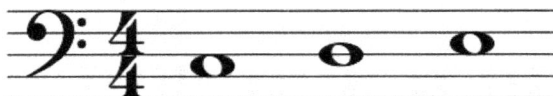

5) Write S for slur or T for tie under each example below.

    S   T   S   S   T

6) Write S under the notes that are staccato and D under the notes that are dotted half notes.

    D   S   S   D

7) Draw Space notes and then write their letter name underneath.

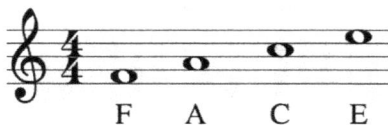

    F   A   C   E

8) Draw line notes and then write their letter name underneath.

    E   G   B   D   F

LESSON 4

1) Draw circle note heads on bass C and draw the first 5 notes of the C scale (C-D-E-F-G)

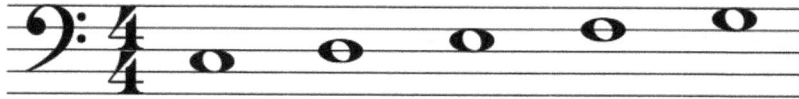

2) What is the note name of the ledger line flashcard image to the right.   C

3) What is the note name of the ledger line flashcard image to the right.   A

4) What is the note name of the ledger line flashcard image to the right   B

5) what is the note name of the ledger line flashcard image to the right.   G

6) What interval is the image to the right showing?

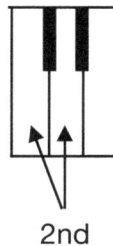

2nd

7) What interval is the image to the right showing?

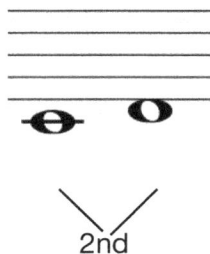

2nd

LESSON 5

1) Draw circle note heads on bass C and draw all 8 of the notes going up the C scale (C-D-E-F-G-A-B-C)

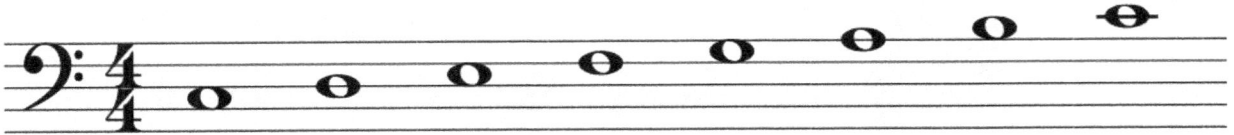

2) In the images below, write H under the half rest and W under the whole rests.

    W   H   W   H

3) What interval is the image to the right showing

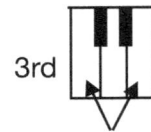

3rd

4) What interval is the image to the right showing

3rd

5) What interval is the image to the right showing

2nd

6) What interval is the image to the right showing

2nd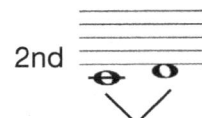

LESSON 6

1) Draw circle note heads on bass C and draw all 8 of the notes going up the C scale (C-D-E-F-G-A-B-C)

2) Draw circle note heads on the MIDDLE C and draw all 8 of the notes going DOWN the C scale

3) On one staff draw the LH C scale going up and going down the staff.

4) Draw an interval of a 2nd up from the note given.

5) Draw an interval of a 3rd up from the note given.

6) Color in the note note on the piano that is a 2nd up from the note the arrow is pointing to.

7) Color in the note on the piano that is a 3rd up from the note the arrow is pointing to.

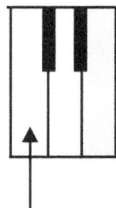

Chapter 2: The G Scale
LESSON 1

1)   Draw the C scale going up and down the scale. Start at bass C, go up to middle C then go back down to bass C.

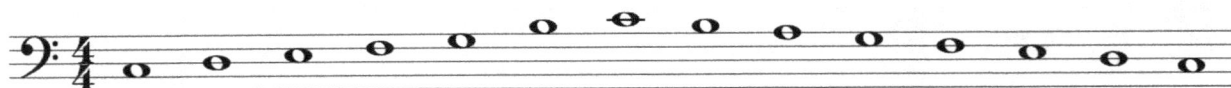

2) Draw the First three notes of the G scale in the Right hand (G-A-B).

3) Draw an interval of a 2nd up from the note given.

4) Draw an interval of a 3rd up from the note given.

5) Draw an interval of a 4th up from the note given

6) Color in the note note on the piano that is a 2nd up from the note the arrow is pointing to.

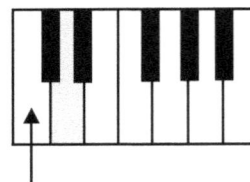

7) Color in the note on the piano that is a 3rd up from the note the arrow is pointing to.

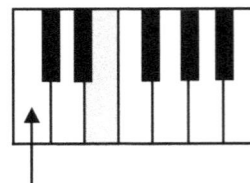

8) Color in the note on the piano that is a 4th up from the note the arrow is pointing to.

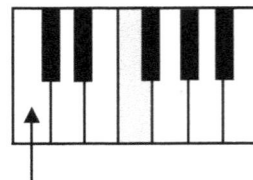

LESSON 2

1) Draw the First four notes of the G scale in the Right hand (G-A-B-C).

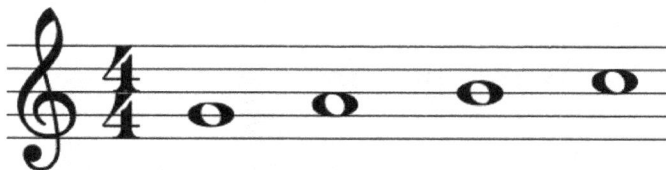

2) Draw an interval of a 2nd up from the note given.

3) Draw an interval of a 3rd up from the note given.

4) Draw an interval of a 4th up from the note given

5) Draw an interval of a 5th up from the note given

6) Color in the note note on the piano that is a 2nd up from the note the arrow is pointing to.

7) Color in the note on the piano that is a 3rd up from the note the arrow is pointing to.

8) Color in the note on the piano that is a 4th up from the note the arrow is pointing to.

10) Color in the note on the piano that is a 5th up from the note the arrow is pointing to.

LESSON 3

1) Draw the First five notes of the G scale in the Right hand (G-A-B-C-D).

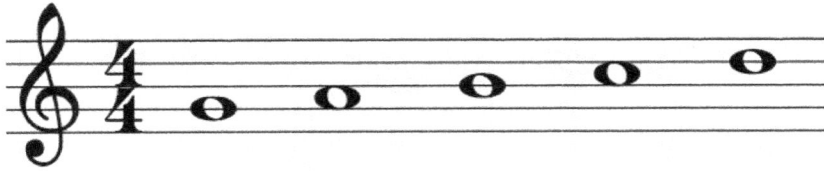

2) What interval is drawn in the image to the right.   2nd

3) What interval is drawn in the image to the right.   5th

4) What interval is drawn in the image to the right   4th

5) What interval is drawn in the image to the right   3rd

6) What interval are the arrows pointing to on the piano image to the right.

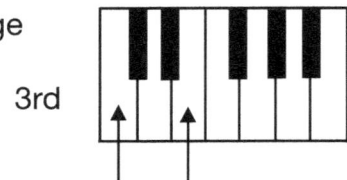

3rd

7) What interval are the arrows pointing to on the piano image to the right.

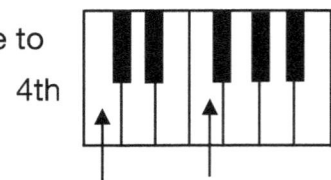

4th

8) What interval are the arrows pointing to on the piano image to the right.

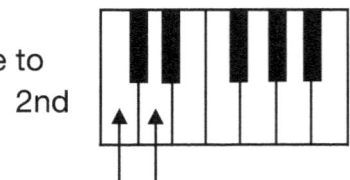

2nd

9) What interval are the arrows pointing to on the piano image to the right.

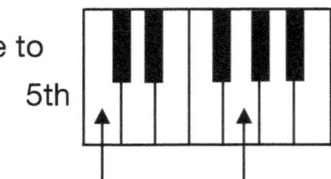

5th

LESSON 4

1) Draw in measure bars. Then Add Staccato notes. Then write in the counts and the letter names. Then play it.

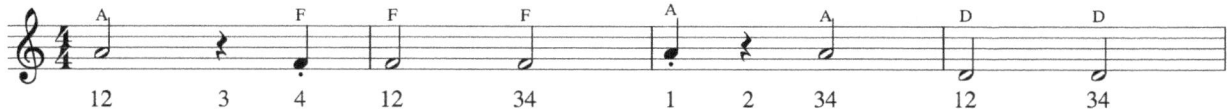

2) Remember the rule we learned that note head stems have to go either up or down and left or right based upon their location on the staff. Using that rule draw the stems correctly on each note head and name the note underneath it.

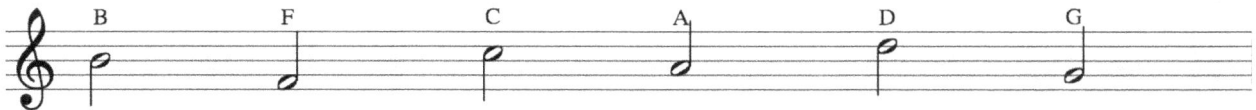

3) Draw the first six notes of the G scale in the Right hand (G-A-B-C-D-E).

4) Draw treble C - D - E - F - G

LESSON 5

1) Draw the stems correctly on each note head and name the note underneath it.

      C   F   D   A   E   C

2) Draw the first seven notes of the G scale in the Right hand (G-A-B-C-D-E-F#). (When drawing a sharp on the staff, the sharp gets drawn BEFORE the note being sharped).

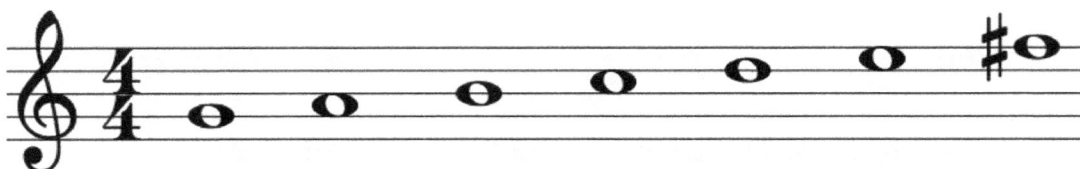

3) Write next to each interval if its a 2nd, 3rd, 4th or 5th

2nd   5th   4th   3rd

4) Write under each interval on the piano if it's a 2nd, 3rd 4th or 5th

   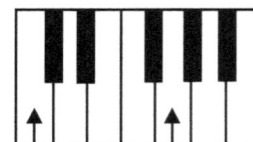

3rd   4th   2nd   5th

LESSON 6

1) Draw the stems correctly on each note head and name the note underneath it.

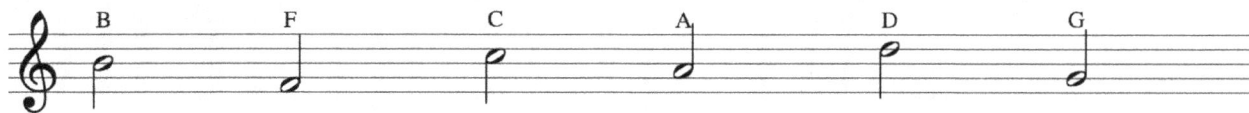

B   F   C   A   D   G

2) Draw all 8 notes of the G scale in the Right hand (G-A-B-C-D-E-F#-G). (When drawing a sharp on the staff, the sharp gets drawn BEFORE the note being sharped).

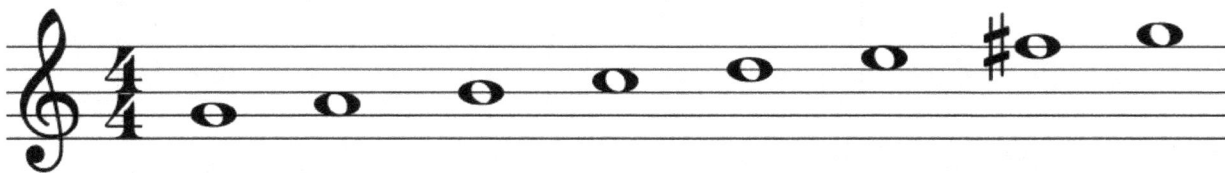

3) Draw in measure bars. Then Add Staccato notes. Then write in the counts and the letter names. Then play it.

A   F   F   F   A   F   D   D

1   2   34   12   34   12   3   4   12   34

4) Draw treble C - D - E - F - G

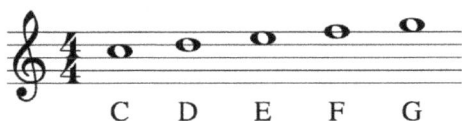

C   D   E   F   G

5) Color the note a 2nd above the note with the arrow

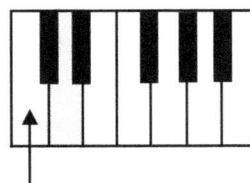

6) Color the note a 5th above the note with the arrow

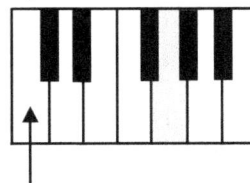

7) Color the note a 4th above the note with the arrow.

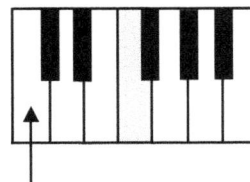

CHAPTER 3: Learning Major Chords
LESSON 1

1) COLOR THE BASS C ON THE PIANO BELOW

MIDDLE C

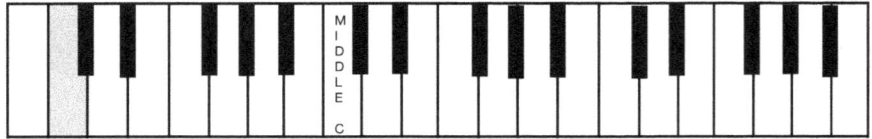

2) COLOR THE TREBLE C ON THE PIANO BELOW

MIDDLE C

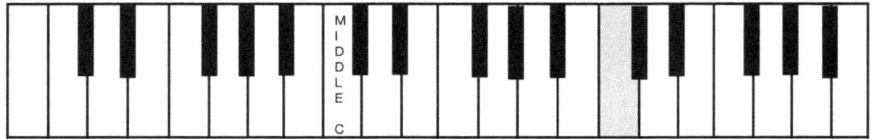

3) COLOR THE NOTES THAT MAKE UP A C MAJOR
CHORD ON THE PIANO TO THE RIGHT.

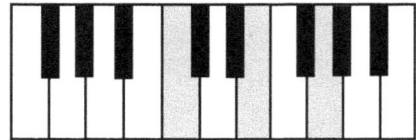

4) BASED ON THE FLASHCARD IMAGE TO THE
RIGHT, COLOR THE SAME NOTE ON THE PIANO BELOW.

MIDDLE

5) BASED ON THE FLASHCARD IMAGE TO THE RIGHT, COLOR THE
SAME NOTE ON THE PIANO BELOW.

MIDDLE

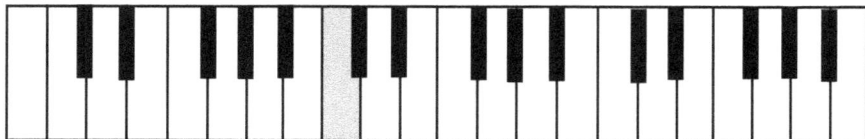

6) BASED ON THE FLASHCARD IMAGE TO THE RIGHT, COLOR THE
SAME NOTE ON   MIDDLE
THE PIANO
BELOW.

LESSON 2

1) Draw all 8 notes in the right hand G scale going up (G-A-B-C-D-E-F#-G). Then draw 1 additional note going down (G-F#)

2) What is the letter name of the ledger line flashcard to the right.   F

3) What is the letter name of the ledger line flashcard to the right.   D

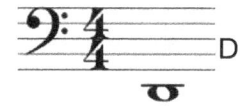

4) What is the letter name of the ledger line flashcard to the right.   E

5) What is the letter name of the ledger line flashcard to the right.   C

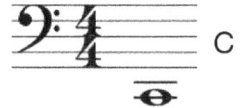

6) Color the note that is an interval of a 3rd above the note with the arrow.

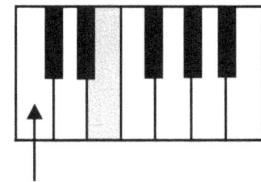

7) Color the note that is an interval of a 5th above the note with the arrow.

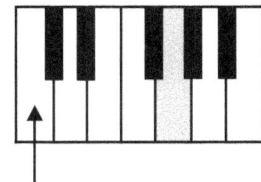

8) Color the note that is an interval of a 4th above the note with the arrow.

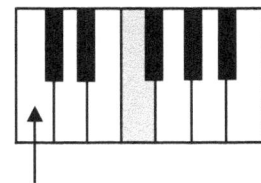

LESSON 3

1) What is the name of the chord drawn on the piano image to the right.

F MAJOR

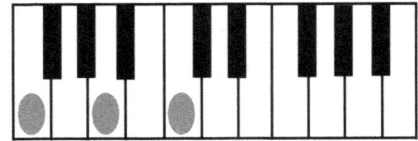

2) What is the name of the chord drawn on the piano image to the right.

C MAJOR

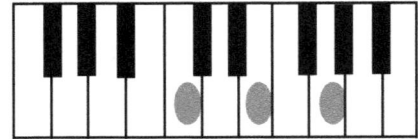

3) Draw all 8 notes in the right hand G scale going up (G-A-B-C-D-E-F#-G). Then draw 2 additional notes going down (G-F#-E)

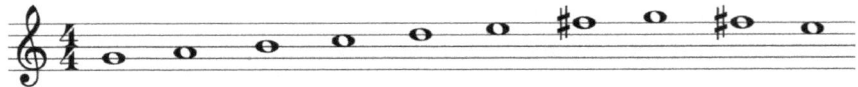

4) Write under each interval if it's a 2nd, 3rd, 4th or 5th.

3rd   5th   4th   2nd

5) Color the notes that make up the F major chord.

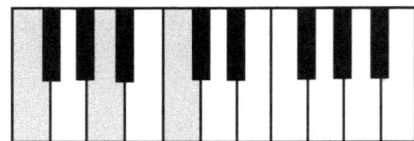

6) Color the notes that make up the C major chord.

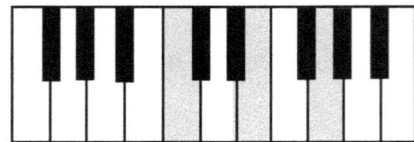

7) Write the letter of each note underneath each flashcard

F   D   E   C

69

LESSON 4

1) Write the letter of each note underneath each flashcard.

E D F D E C

2) Draw all 8 notes in the right hand G scale going up and 3 note going down (G-A-B-C-D-E-F#-G). Then draw 3 additional notes going down (G-F#-E-D).

3) Draw the stems correctly on each note head and name the note underneath it.

C F D A E C

4) Draw in measure bars. Then Add Staccato notes. Then write in the counts and the letter names. Then play it.

1 2 34 | 1 234 | 1 2 34 | 1 2 34

LESSON 5

1) Draw all 8 notes in the right hand G scale going up (G-A-B-C-D-E-F#-G). Then draw 5 additional notes going down (G-F#-E-D-C-B).

2) 2) Color the notes that make up the C Major chord.

3) Color the notes that make up the F Major chord.

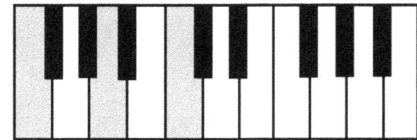

4) Color the notes that make up the G Major chord.

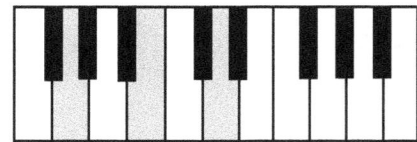

5) Color the note that is an interval of a 3rd above the note with the arrow.

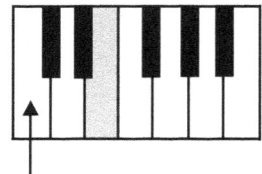

6) Color the note that is an interval of a 5th above the note with the arrow.

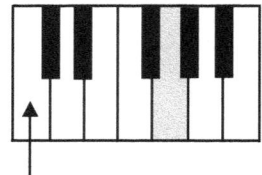

7) Color the note that is an interval of a 4th above the note with the arrow.

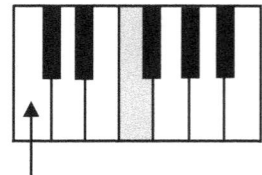

8) Color the note that is an interval of a 2nd above the note with the arrow.

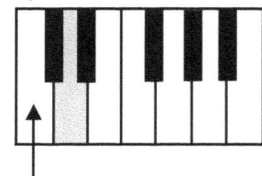

71

LESSON 6

1) Draw all 8 notes in the right hand G scale going up and 3 note going down (G-A-B-C-D-E-F#-G). Then draw all 8 notes going down (G-F#-E-D-C-B-A-G).

2) Write the letter of each note underneath each flashcard.

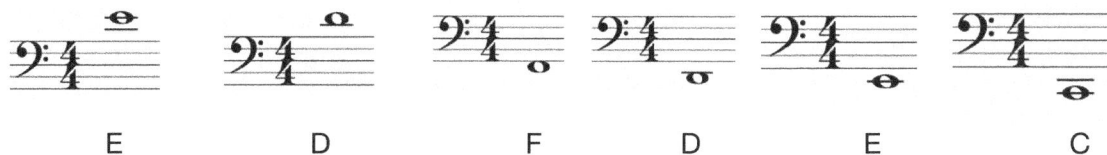

E   D   F   D   E   C

3) Write the name of the chord you see drawn on the piano image to the right

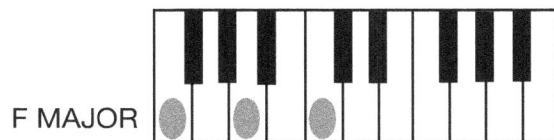

F MAJOR

4) Write the name of the chord you see drawn on the piano image to the right

C MAJOR

5) Write the name of the chord you see drawn on the piano image to the right

G MAJOR

6) In the images below write H under the half rests and W under the whole rests.

W   H   W   H

CHAPTER 4: More Major Chords and Playing 8va.
LESSON 1

1) Circle on the piano image a C#

2) Circle on the piano image a F#

3) Circle on the piano image a D #

4) Circle on the piano image an A #

5) Circle on the piano image a B-flat

6) Circle on the piano image a D-flat

7) Circle on the piano image a G-flat

8) Circle on the piano image an A-flat

LESSON 2

1) Write the C major scale going up and down the scale

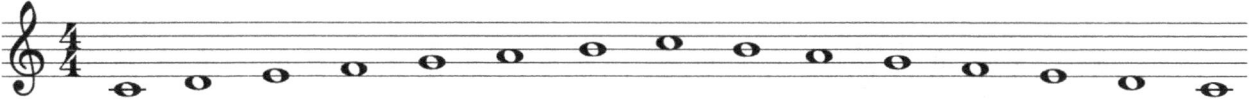

2) Write the G major scale going up and down the scale

3) Color the note on the piano below in the correct location that the music shows

4) Color the note on the piano below in the correct location that the music shows

5) Color the note on the piano below in the correct location that the music shows

6) Draw a C major chord on the staff. Remember the bottom note should be the name of the chord and then the rest of the chord is skips.

LESSON 3

1) Color the note on the piano below in the correct location that the music shows

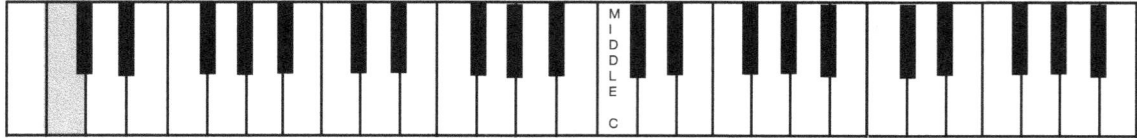

2) Color the note on the piano below in the correct location that the music shows

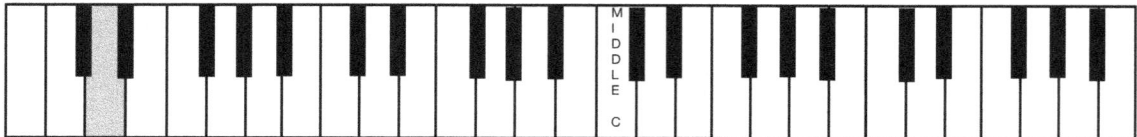

3) Color the note on the piano below in the correct location that the music shows

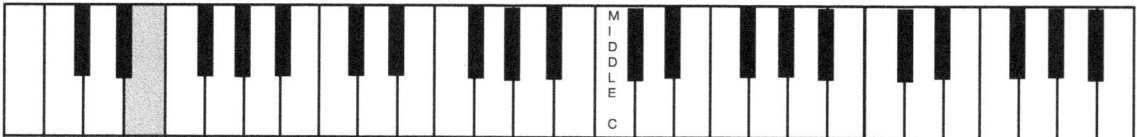

4) Draw a whole rest in each measure (Remember the whole rest hangs down from the 4th line

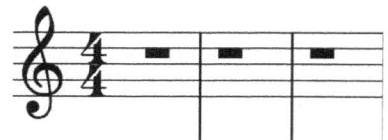

5) Draw two half rests in each measure (Remember the half rest sits above the 3rd line)

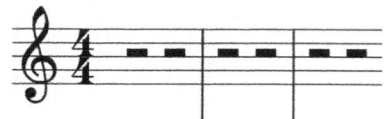

6) Draw a F major chord on the staff. Remember the bottom note should be the name of the chord and then the rest of the chord is skips

75

LESSON 4

1) Color the note on the piano below in the correct location in the music.

2) Color the note on the piano below in the correct location that the music shows.

3) Color the note on the piano below in the correct location that the music shows.

4) Draw whole rests in each measures with the treble clef (Remember the whole rest hangs down from the 4th line)
and two half rests in each measure in the bass clef (Remember the half rest sits above the 3rd line)

5) Draw a G major chord on the staff. Remember the bottom note should be the name of the chord and then the rest of the chord is skips

LESSON 5

1) Identify the name of the chord you see drawn in the image to the right

F MAJOR

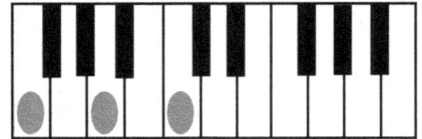

2) Identify the name of the chord you see drawn in the image to the right

C MAJOR

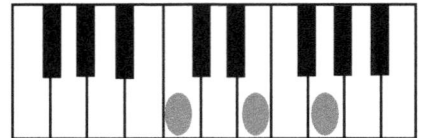

3) Identify the name of the chord you see drawn in the image to the right

G MAJOR

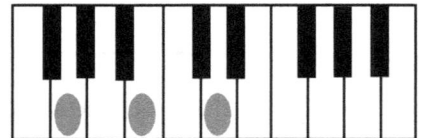

4) Identify the name of the chord you see drawn in the image to the right

D MAJOR

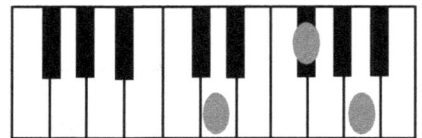

5) Identify the name of the chord you see drawn in the image to the right

E MAJOR

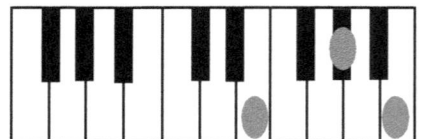

6) Identify the name of the chord you see drawn in the image to the right

A MAJOR

CHAPTER 5: Playing Sharps and Flats
LESSON 1

1) What are the black notes if any in the C scale? **NONE**

2) What are the black notes if any in the G scale? **F#**

3) What are the black notes in the D scale? **F#, C#**

4) Draw the first 2 notes in the right hand D scale going up (D-E)

5) Color the note on the piano image to the right that is an interval of a 3rd BELOW the note with the arrow.

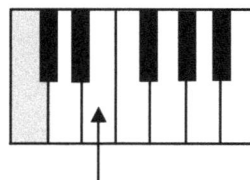

6) Color the note on the piano image to the right that is an interval of a 5th BELOW the note with the arrow.

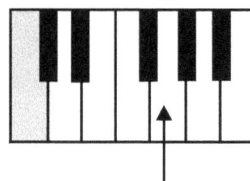

7) Color the note on the piano image to the right that is an interval of a 4th BELOW the note with the arrow.

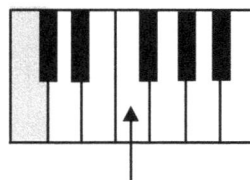

8) Color the note on the piano image to the right that is an interval of a 2nd BELOW the note with the arrow.

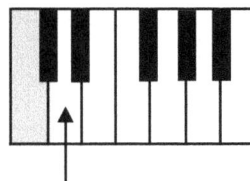

LESSON 2

1) What scale has 2 black notes? **D**

2) What scale has 0 black notes? **C**

3) what scale has 1 black notes? **G**

4) Draw the first 3 notes in the right hand D scale going up (D-E-F#)

5) Draw a note an interval of a 2nd DOWN from the note in the image to the right.

6) Draw a note an interval of a 5th DOWN from the note in the image to the right.

7) Draw a note an interval of a 3rd DOWN from the note in the image to the right.

8) Draw a note an interval of a 4th DOWN from the note in the image to the right.

LESSON 3

1) What scale has the black note F#? **G**

2) What scale has no black notes? **C**

3) What scale has the black notes F# **and** C#? **D**

4) Draw the first 5 notes on the RH D scale going up (D-E-F#-G-A)

5) Draw in the missing sharps (#) in the scale drawn below. Remember when we draw a sharp on a staff it comes BEFORE the note being sharped.

6) Color the note on the piano below in the correct location that the music shows.

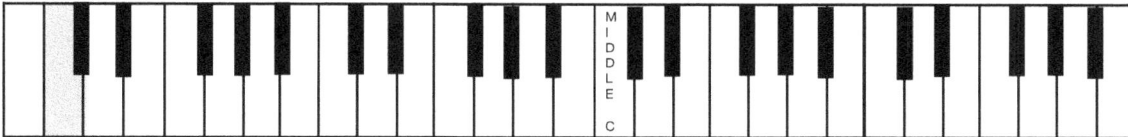

7) Color the note on the piano below in the correct location that the music shows.

LESSON 4

1) What scale is written in the image below? **G SCALE**

2) Write the name of the note underneath each flashcard.

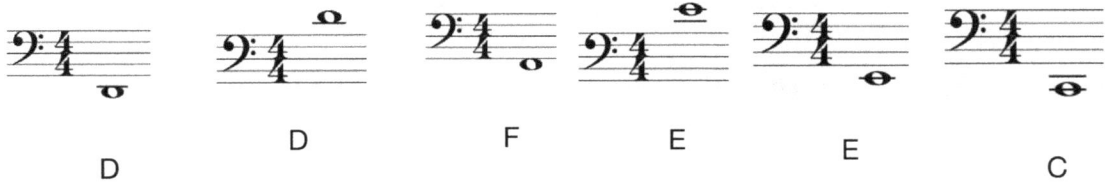

D   D   F   E   E   C

3) Draw the first 6 notes of the RH D scale going up (D-E-F#-G-A-B)

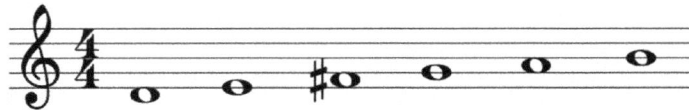

4 6) Circle on the piano image a D #

7) Circle on the piano image a A flat

8) Circle on the piano image an G#

81

LESSON 5

1) What scale is written in the image below? **C SCALE**

2) Circle on the piano image a G-flat

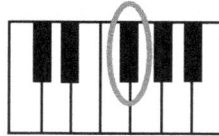

2) Circle on the piano image a F#

3) Circle on the piano image a E-flat

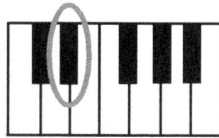

4) Circle on the piano image an A #

5) Circle on the piano image a B-flat

6) Draw the first 7 notes of the RH D scale going up (D-E-F#-G-A-B-C#).

LESSON 6

1) What scale is written in the image below? **D SCALE**

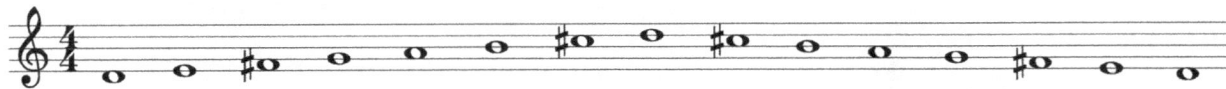

2) Identify the name of the chord you see drawn in the image to the right. **D MAJOR CHORD**

2) Identify the name of the chord you see drawn in the image to the right. **C MAJOR CHORD**

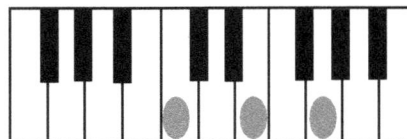

3) Identify the name of the chord you see drawn in the image to the right. **A MAJOR CHORD**

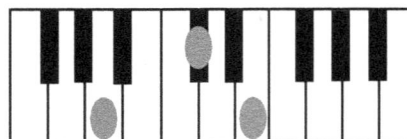

4) Identify the name of the chord you see drawn in the image to the right. **F MAJOR CHORD**

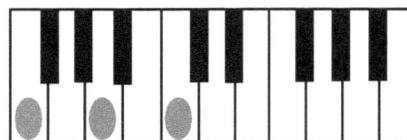

5) Identify the name of the chord you see drawn in the image to the right. **E MAJOR CHORD**

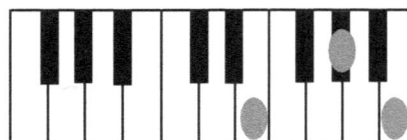

6) Identify the name of the chord you see drawn in the image to the right. **G MAJOR CHORD**

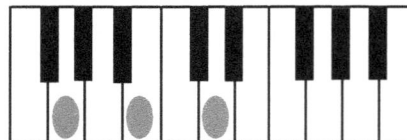

7) Draw all 8 notes of the RH D scale going up (D-E-F#-G-A-B-C#-D)

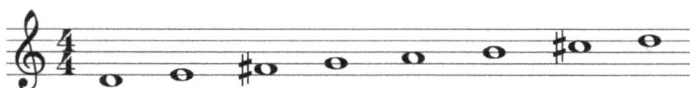

CHAPTER 6: Playing Chords in Music
LESSON 1

1) Shade in the notes in the correct location on the piano below the chord in the image to the right.

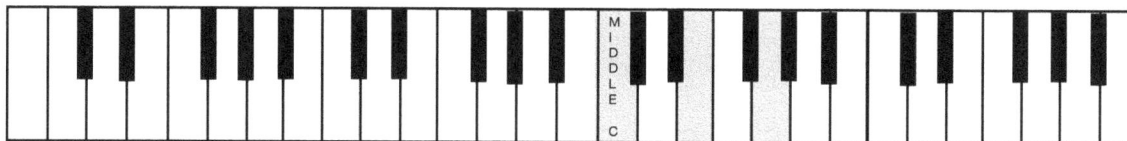

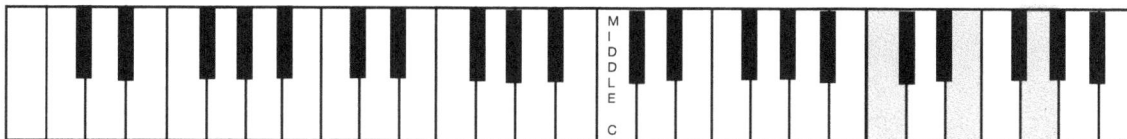

2) Shade in the notes in the correct location on the piano below the chord in the image to the right.

3). Draw all 8 notes in the right hand D scale going up (D-E-F#-G-A-B-C#-D). Then draw 1 additional note going down (D-C#).

4) Write the name of each note underneath the note.

F#   A#   C#   G#   D#   F#

LESSON 2

1) Shade in the notes in the correct location on the piano below the chord in the image to the right.

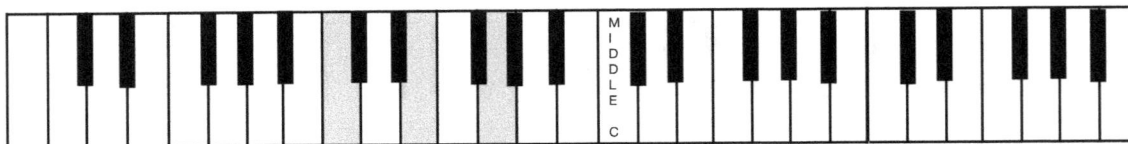

2) Shade in the notes in the correct location on the piano below the chord in the image to the right.

3) Draw all 8 notes in the right hand D scale going up (D-E-F#-G-A-B-C#-D). Then draw 3 additional notes going down (D-C#-B-A).

4) Write the name of each note underneath the note.

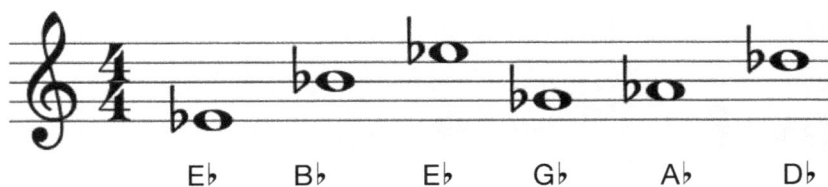

Eb   Bb   Eb   Gb   Ab   Db

85

LESSON 3

1) Shade in the notes in the correct location on the piano below the chord in the image to the right.

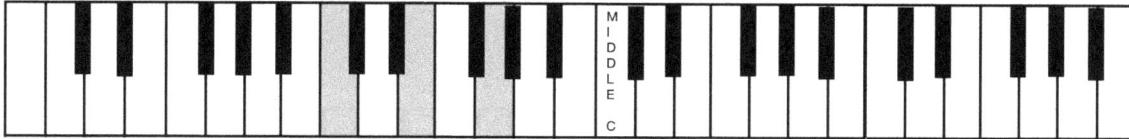

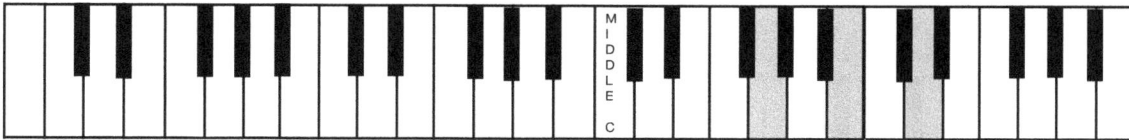

2) Shade in the notes in the correct location on the piano below the chord in the image to the right.

3) Draw all 8 notes in the right hand D scale going up (D-E-F#-G-A-B-C#-D). Then draw 5 additional notes going down (D-C#-B-A-G-F#).

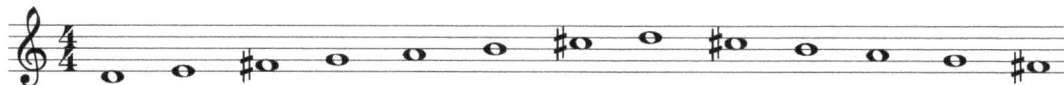

4) Draw the note that gets 1 beat __ 𝅘𝅥 _____   9) Draw a quarter note _ 𝅘𝅥 _____

5). Draw the note that gets 4 beats_____   10) Draw a half note ___ 𝅗𝅥 _____

6) Draw the note that gets 3 beats _____   11) Draw a whole note _____

7) Draw the note that gets 2 beats _____ 𝅗𝅥 ____   12) Draw a quarter rest ____ 𝄽 ____

LESSON 4

1) Shade in the notes in the correct location on the piano below the chord in the image to the right.

2) Shade in the notes in the correct location on the piano below the chord in the image to the right.

3) Draw all 8 notes in the right hand D scale going up (D-E-F#-G-A-B-C#-D). Then draw all 8 additional notes going down (D-C#-B-A-G-F#-E-D).

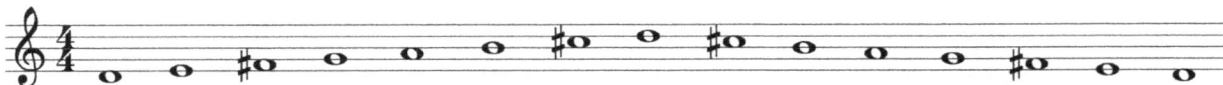

4) Draw in measure bars. Then Add Staccato notes. Then write in the counts and the letter names. Then play it.

D   F   C   E   C   G   C

1 2 34   1 2 34   1 2 3 4   1 2 3 4

LESSON 5

1) Shade in the notes in the correct location on the piano below the chord in the image to the right.

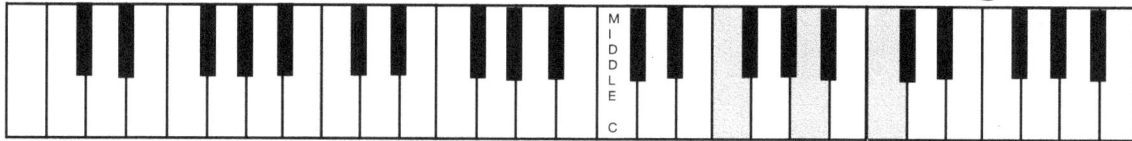

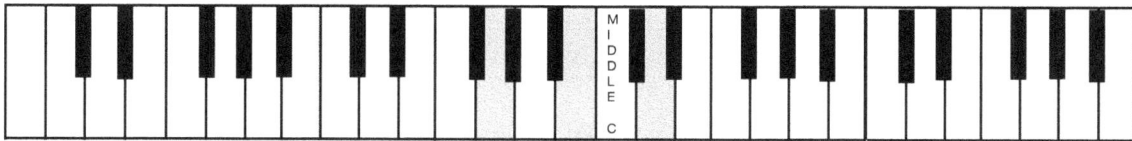

2) Shade in the notes in the correct location on the piano below the chord in the image to the right.

3) Draw the C scale going up and Down in the right hand. Underneath each note write the finger number that plays that note.

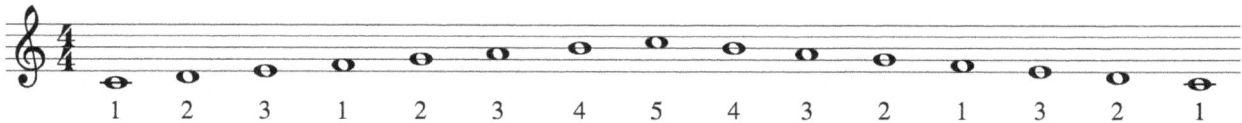

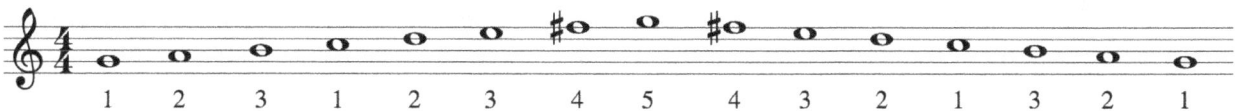

1 2 3 1 2 3 4 5 4 3 2 1 3 2 1

4) Draw that G scale going up and Down in the right hand. Underneath each note write the finger number that plays that note.

1 2 3 1 2 3 4 5 4 3 2 1 3 2 1

5) Draw the D scale going up and down in the right hand. Underneath each note write the finger number that plays that note.

1 2 3 1 2 3 4 5 4 3 2 1 3 2 1

LESSON 6

1) Shade in the notes in the correct location on the piano below the chord in the image to the right.

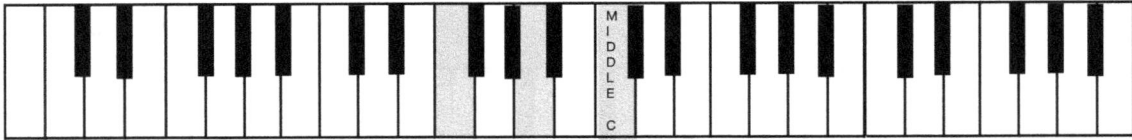

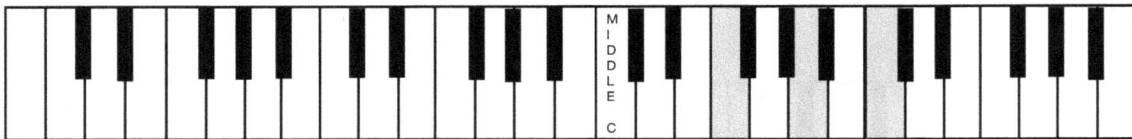

2) Shade in the notes in the correct location on the piano below the chord in the image to the right.

3) Draw the C scale going up and Down in the left hand. Underneath each note write the finger number that plays that note.

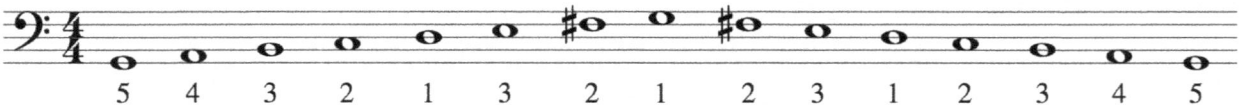

5   4   3   2   1   3   2   1   2   3   1   2   3   4   5

4) Draw that G scale going up and Down in the left hand. Underneath each note write the finger number that plays that note.

5   4   3   2   1   3   2   1   2   3   1   2   3   4   5

5) Add measure bars. Draw in staccato note where applicable. Then write in the counts and letter names and play it.

D   C   E   D   F G   C

12 3 4   1 2 3 4   1 2 3 4   1 2 3 4

89

CHAPTER 7: Practicing Major Chords
LESSON 1

1) Draw the stems correctly on each note head and write the note name underneath it.

C   F   D   A   E   C

2) Identify in each image below if it is an interval of a 2nd, 3rd, 4th or 5th. Than play that interval on the piano.

3rd   4th   2nd   5th

3) Identify the interval indicated by the arrows on each piano below (2nd, 3rd, 4th, 5th).

5th   2nd   4th   3rd

4) Draw the first 3 notes in the F Scale in the RH going up (F-G-A).

5) Draw in the missing bar lines. Write in the counts and note names. Play the song on the piano.

C   E   G   F   E

12 3 | 1 2 3 | 1 2 3 | 1 23 | 123

LESSON 2

1) Draw an interval of a 4th going up starting from a D note.

2) Draw an interval of a 3rd going up starting from a F note. (There are two locations the answer could have been drawn. Either location is correct).

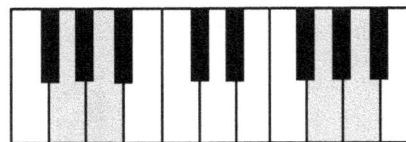

3) Draw an interval of a 5th going up starting from a E note.

4) Draw an interval of a 2nd going up starting from a G note (there are two locations the answer could have been drawn. Either location is correct).

5) Draw the stems correctly on each note head and write the note name underneath it.

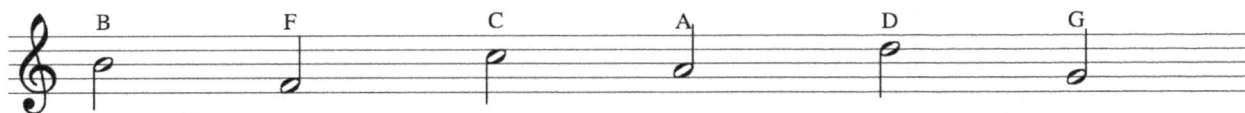

B　　　　F　　　　C　　　　A　　　　D　　　　G

6) Draw the first 4 notes of the F scale in the RH going up (F-G-A-B ♭).

LESSON 3

1) Draw an interval of a 3rd up from the note in the image to the right then play the two notes on a piano.

2) Draw an interval of a 4th up from the note in the image to the right then play the two notes on a piano.

3) Draw an interval of a 2nd up from the note in the image to the right then play the two notes on a piano.

4) Draw an interval of a 5th up from the note in the image to the right then play the two notes on a piano.

5) Draw the first 5 notes of the F scale in the RH going up (F-G-A-B♭-C).

6) Draw in the missing bar lines. Write the counts and note names. Play the music.

LESSON 4

1) What is the interval you see drawn in the image to the right?

4th

2) What is the interval you see drawn in the image to the right?

5th

3) What is the interval you see drawn in the image to the right?

2nd

4) What is the interval you see drawn in the image to the right?

3rd

5) Draw all 8 notes of the F scale in the RH going up (F-G-A-B♭-C-D-E-F).

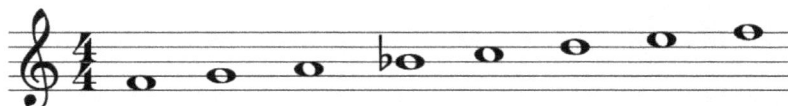

6) Draw in the missing bar lines. Write in the counts and note names. Play the music.

LESSON 5

1) Draw all 8 notes of the F scale in the RH going up (F-G-A-B ♭ -C-D-E-F), then draw 3 additional notes going down (E-D-C).

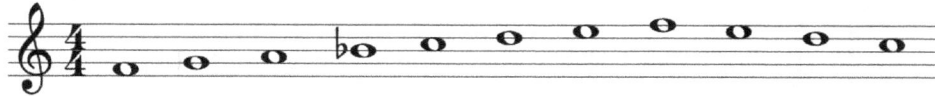

2) Write the note name of the flashcard in each image below.

C   E   D   D   E   F

3) Write the note name of the flashcard in each image below.

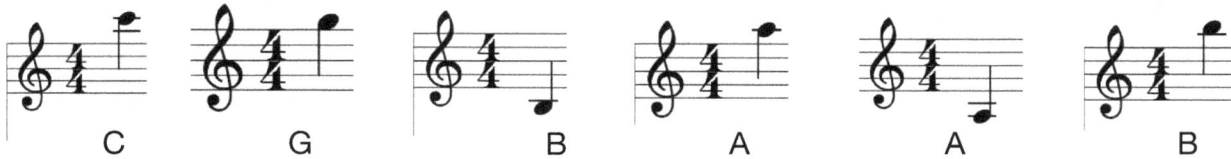

C   G   B   A   A   B

4) Draw an interval of a 2nd down from the note in the image to the right. Then play the two notes on the piano.

5) Draw an interval of a 3rd down from the note in the image to the right. Then play the two notes on the piano.

6) Draw an interval of a 5th down from the note In the image to the right. Then play the two notes on the piano.

7) Draw an interval of a 4th down from the note in the image to the right. Then play the two notes on the piano.

LESSON 6

1) Draw all 8 notes of the F scale in the RH going up (F-G-A-B♭-C-D-E-F), then draw 4 additional notes going down (E-D-C-B♭).

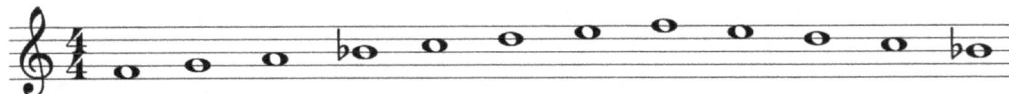

2) Color the white notes and circle any black notes in a C chord

3) Color the white notes and circle any black notes in a D Chord

4) Color the white notes and circle any black notes in an E chord

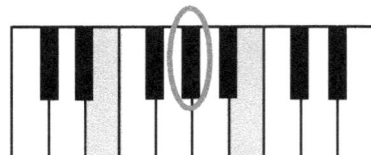

5) Color the notes in a F chord

6) Color the notes in a G chord

7) Color the notes in an A chord.

CHAPTER 8: Putting It All Together
LESSON 1

1) Draw all 8 notes of the F scale in the RH going up (F-G-A-B♭-C-D-E-F), then draw all 8 notes going down (F- E-D-C-B♭-A-G-F).

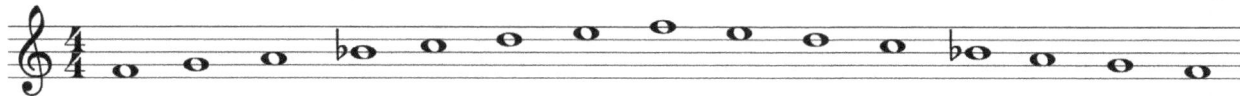

2) On the piano below, color the note in the correct location that the LH would play and draw an arrow pointing to the correct location that the RH would play.

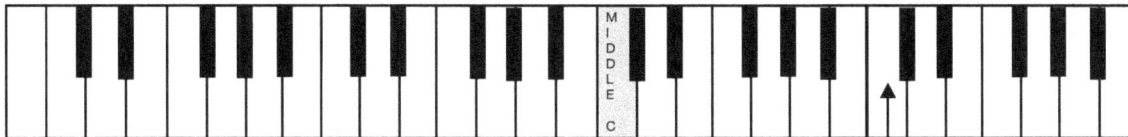

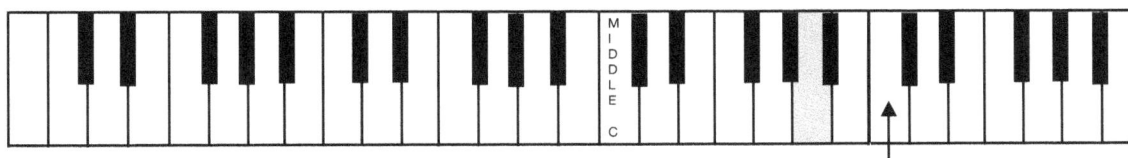

3) On the piano below, color the note in the correct location that the LH would play and draw an arrow pointing to the correct location that the RH would play.

4) On the piano below, color the note in the correct location that the LH would play and draw an arrow pointing to the correct location that the RH would play.

LESSON 2

1) On the piano below, color the note in the correct location that the LH would play and draw an arrow pointing to the correct location that the RH would play based on the image to the right.

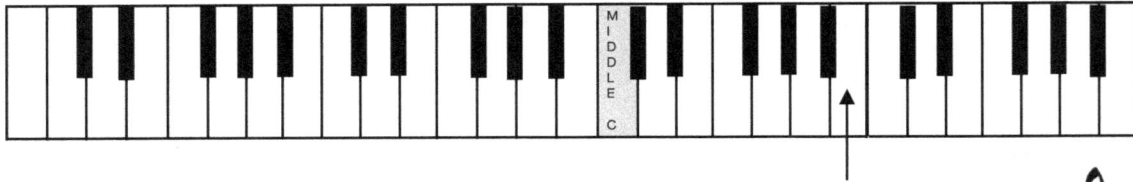

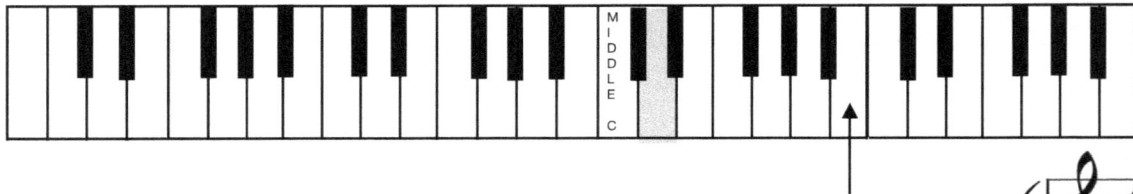

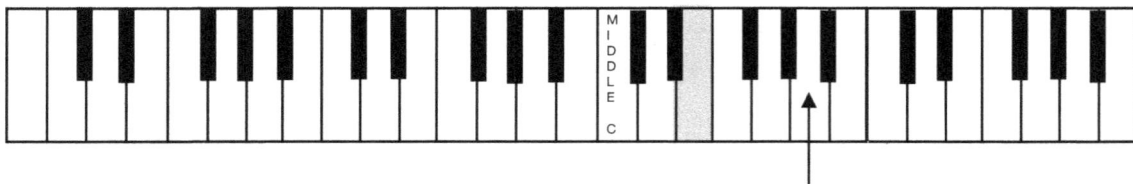

2) On the piano below, color the note in the correct location that the LH would play and draw an arrow pointing to the correct location that the RH would play based on the image to the right.

3) On the piano below, color the note in the correct location that the LH would play and draw an arrow pointing to the correct location that the RH would play based on the image to the right.

4) Draw a F scale in the RH going up and down. Include the   finger numbers on each note.

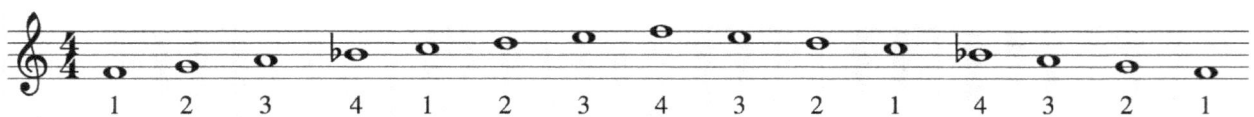

1   2   3   4   1   2   3   4   3   2   1   4   3   2   1

LESSON 3

1) Draw a C scale in the RH going up and down with finger numbers underneath.

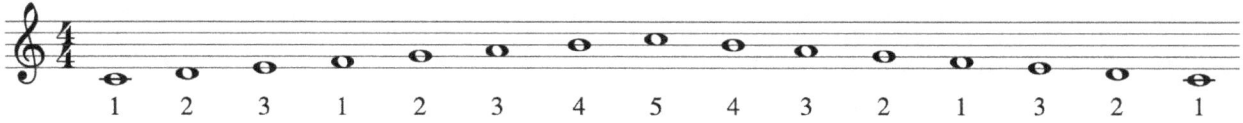

1 2 3 1 2 3 4 5 4 3 2 1 3 2 1

2) Draw a G scale in the RH going up and down with the finger numbers underneath.

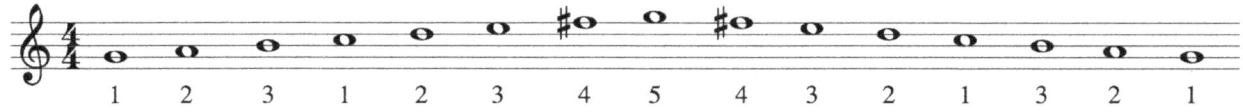

1 2 3 1 2 3 4 5 4 3 2 1 3 2 1

3) Draw a D scale in the RH going up and down with the finger numbers underneath.

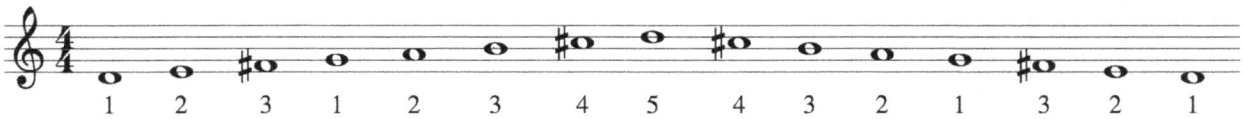

1 2 3 1 2 3 4 5 4 3 2 1 3 2 1

4) Draw a F scale in the RH going up and down with the finger numbers underneath.

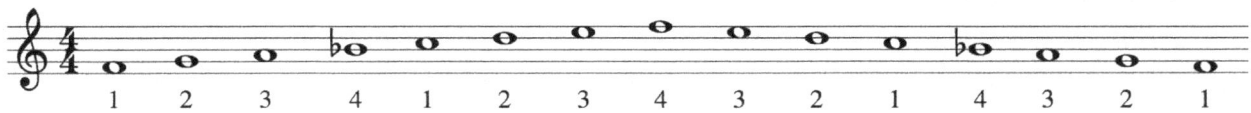

1 2 3 4 1 2 3 4 3 2 1 4 3 2 1

5) Color the correct location on the piano for the image to the right.

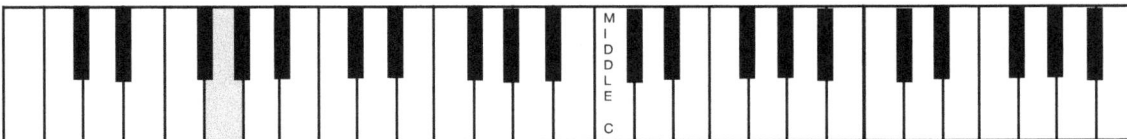

6) Color the correct location on the piano for the image to the right.

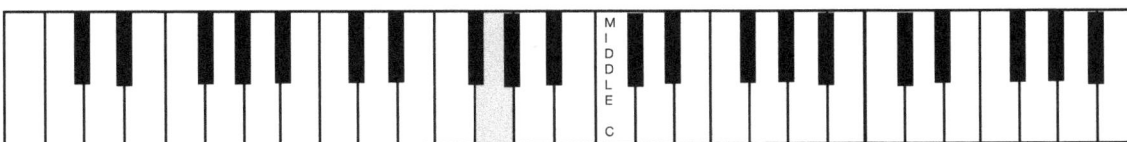

LESSON 4

1) What if any are the black notes in the D Scale? **F#, C#**

2) What if any are the black notes in the C scale? **NONE**

3) What if any are the black notes in the G scale? **F#**

4) What if any are the black notes in the F scale? **B ♭**

5) What three major chords use all white notes? **C, F, G**

6) What three major chords have a black note in the middle? **D, E, A**

7) What major chord uses 2 black notes? **B**

8) What does Rit. Stand for and what is its definition? **RITARDANDO; TO GRADUALLY DECREASE IN SPEED.**

9) Draw a fermata and give its definition. ⌢ **HOLD A NOTE EXTRA LONG**

10) What term does *mp* stand for and what does it mean? *MEZZO PIANO; MODERATELY/MEDIUM SOFT*

11) Draw a whole rest and tell how many beats. ▬ **4 beats.**

12) Draw a half rest and tell how many beats. ▬ **2 beats.**

13) What does 8va mean? **TO PLAY AN OCTAVE HIGHER OR LOWER**

14) What are the notes in a C major chord? **C-E-G**

15) What are the notes in a D major chord? **D-F#-A**

16) What are the notes in an E major chord? **E-G#-B**

17) What are the notes in a F major chord? **F-A-C**

18) What are the notes in a G major chord? **G-B-D**

19) What are the notes in an A major chord? **A-C#-E**

20) What are the notes in a B major chord? **B-D#-F#**

Other Resources From This Author:

Join the Parker Music Academy
Online Community

Free resources, Online Course, Community
of like-minded parents and teachers and more.

parkermusicacademy.us

About The Author:

Stephanie Parker has played classical piano for over 35 years. She attended Florida State University College of Music with a concentration in piano. She has been teaching piano for over 20 years as well as been a homeschooling mom since 2006. Homeschooling her children has given her a unique skill set to learn how to teach effectively mainly age ranges with many differing abilities. It has also shown her parents are very capable of teaching their children many subjects with the proper help which is why she wants to create this book to help parents who want to give the gift of music to their child, but may not have the time or money to do so.